Books by Ernest A. Fitzgerald

GOD WRITES STRAIGHT WITH CROOKED LINES

(*1981*)

HOW TO BE A SUCCESSFUL FAILURE   (*1978*)

God Writes Straight
with Crooked Lines

DR. ERNEST A. FITZGERALD

God Writes Straight with Crooked Lines

New York   1981   ATHENEUM

Library of Congress Cataloging in Publication Data

Fitzgerald, Ernest A.
   God writes straight with crooked lines.

      1. Christian life—Methodist authors.
I. Title.
BV4501.2.F52   1981   248.4'87   80-65997
ISBN 0-689-11073-1

Published simultaneously in Canada by
McClelland and Stewart, Ltd.
Manufactured by American Book-Stratford Press, Inc.
Saddle Brook, New Jersey
Designed by Kathleen Carey
First Edition

To Elizabeth and David Lewis

With Appreciation

M Y deep gratitude is extended to the members of Centenary United Methodist Church in Winston-Salem, North Carolina, who allow me to speak each Sunday to thousands of people both in person and by means of radio; to my wife, Frances, and my secretary, Mrs. David Lewis, who constantly challenge me to address the issues; and to Mrs. Walter E. Johnston, Jr., who did the initial proofreading. I am especially indebted to Fisher-Harrison, Inc., publishers of *Pace*, the in-flight magazine of Piedmont Airlines, for permission to reprint some of the material I have used in my regular columns and in their other publications.

Foreword

H E was perched on the ledge of a building forty
stories above a busy street in New York City. A
crowd had gathered on the adjacent corner below,
their eyes fixed on the man as he careened crazily
back and forth between two open windows. The
people knew the man would probably fall or jump
before the police could race up the elevator to him.
Even if the officers reached the windows in time,
no one knew whether the man could be persuaded
to come inside. According to a reporter who was
present, a young Catholic priest had been pressed

into service. His task was to convince the man that life was still worth living. The story of that young priest's successful adventure was in the nation's newspapers a while back.

The reporter who wrote the story asked the priest, "What did you tell him?" Have you ever wondered what you would say if you were confronted with such a situation? Fortunately, most of us will be spared that kind of experience. People walking the ledges of high buildings in full view of a city are few indeed. Yet almost every newspaper in our land will carry a story of someone who has been driven to despair by the overwhelming pressures of our times. And for every story of someone who makes the final leap, there are thousands of other people who don't take the "big exit." They live out their lives, as the poet declared, "in quiet desperation." But the question these people ask is always the same: "How do you manage to live in a world where every day is spent in the pressure-cooker, and you have to find directions when the signposts are down?"

Anyone who spends much time behind the counselor's desk keeps running into that question. As the shock waves of change roll across our world, the intensity of the inquiry increases. Most people, regardless of the masks they wear, are up against it in a rough-and-tumble world. Surely some word of hope to these people would be appropriate. This volume is offered in the sincere hope it will make the journey a little less rugged for someone.

By design the chapters are brief. They may be read quickly by people who are on the run and don't have the time to plow through the countless pages of current "how-to" books. The author has a few dreams, however. It is my hope that these pages deal with real-life situations. I would hope, too, that they may offer some word of encouragement to those who live on "the ragged edge of despair." For those who are well-adjusted and happy, perhaps this book will serve as a reinforcement for the dark days that come to us all.

Contents

Contents

God Writes Straight
with Crooked Lines

Searching for the Signposts

STRUGGLING WITH LIFE'S DIRECTIONS

O N a December morning in 1944, the eyes of the free world focused on a battle line a hundred miles inside the Belgian border. The Allied offensive, begun six months before, had rolled with relentless precision across Western Europe. Suddenly, on that December day, a major portion of the mighty juggernaut ground to a halt. A counter-offensive had been launched, and a great bulge in the battle lines became apparent. It was a critical day for Allied soldiers. If the counter-offensive had succeeded, the end of the war might have been indefinitely delayed. The drive almost succeeded, and a part of the reason for its success was some brilliant strategy devised by the defenders of the Third Reich.

A few days before, German soldiers dressed in American uniforms, together with American jeeps, had been parachuted behind American lines. These "soldiers from the sky" carried no weapons. Their mission was to drive the roads over which reinforcing Allied armies might travel and change all signs pointing to strategic towns and villages. Their task of turning the signposts to give wrong directions had deadly consequences. The defenders in the "Battle of the Bulge" called for help, but much of the needed help never arrived. Whole battalions were lost, trying to find their way across a countryside where the signposts were either down or wrong.

The story of those critical days was related recently by one of America's leading churchmen, Dr. Lee F. Tuttle. Those who listened to Dr. Tuttle could not help but reflect on how nearly those events parallel life in contemporary times. The confusion of an age in transition makes most of us see life as a forced march over uncharted terrain.

The other day an industrial psychologist stated that the average businessman in this decade feels harassed and frayed, driven by too many things to do and too little time in which to accomplish them.

4

Adding to his dilemma are the pressures of problems of unprecedented magnitude. That description encompasses far more people than those who sit at desks in America's corporations. Included in the list must be homemakers, students, professionals, industrial workers, politicians, athletes, and even those who are retired. We travel at a dizzy pace, not always sure of direction. We keep looking for the signposts, hoping for help in finding our way.

Any counselor meets daily with such people, who always ask the same question: "How does one find direction when someone has tampered with the signs?" No competent counselor, however, is ever deceived by that question. What people are really asking is, "How can one find a meaningful life in a pressurized world where one always feels pushed and shoved?" The answer to that question needs to be examined in the light of specific situations, and that's what this book is about. There are, however, some overriding principles that must be considered if there is to be any tranquillity in these troubled times.

We need to remember, for instance, that a philosophy of life is imperative if we are to weather impending storms. A few years ago the U.S. Chamber of Commerce sponsored a study on what might happen in America over the next thirty years. The study was designed to aid business heads in planning for the future. For the most part the report was optimistic. The predictions, based on what was happening when the study was done, appeared reasonable. At the beginning of the report, however, the point was made that talking about the future is a risky business. As we do long-range thinking, we must keep in mind the possibility of such calamities as depressions, global wars, and other national or international problems that could upset more hopeful speculations.

This thought suggests one of the basic problems of our times. If predicting the future required nothing more than an analysis of existing circumstances and following them to their logical conclusions, then forecasting what lies ahead would be a simple procedure. The trouble, however, is that the future is always subject to the unforeseen. We live in a time when the unexpected happens daily. This is one reason we suffer so much apprehension and anxiety. Who knows what kind of world we will have tomorrow?

Someone has said that eighty percent of the jobs that will be available in the next twenty years do not exist today. This seems incredible but, if it's true, it could explain a part of our restlessness. Imagine trying to train for a vocation the demands of which are unknown while we are training for it.

Yet to some degree this is a parable for all of life in our generation. Life keeps moving us into strange lands, and there are no signs. If we are to maintain any balance in our world, we must have regulating points of view—convictions about life that will hold together no matter what happens.

One of the oldest stories in the world is about a couple of carpenters who set out to build their homes. One of the men was a wise builder. He dug deep and anchored his house on the rock. The other builder, a man in a hurry, took no time for digging and laid his foundations on the sand. One day an unexpected storm swept the area. The wise builder found himself enjoying the security of a well-built house. The other man was left standing in the rain.

The lesson of that story is so incredibly simple we often miss it. In a world of the unexpected, the only way to stand steady is to be tied to something. The wise builder knew that. There is no way to know when the storm will come. If the house is going to withstand the rain, you get ready in the sunshine. A long time ago someone summed up the point of this story in a simple sentence: "If you do what you are supposed to do today, tomorrow you will come out where you are supposed to be." That's one signpost no one can afford to miss.

There is a second prerequisite for living under

pressure in a trackless world. We must establish a moral framework against which we make our decisions.

A sportswriter recently reported that from the time the ball leaves the pitcher's hand, a batter has one-third of a second to decide if he will swing. That's the way most choices come at us in this runaway world. The alternatives pounce upon us and demand immediate decisions. You can't ponder the options forever; you have to decide and move on. However, no one ever successfully handles immediate decisions unless he has made some prior decisions. Those prior decisions have to do with what we truly believe is consistent with God's scheme for life.

It is said that Johann Sebastian Bach wrote music for instruments that in his time had not been invented. If we extrapolate from that, a much wider possibility is suggested: tomorrow we may have to make judgments that will have far-reaching impact on our lives. It will relieve a lot of pressure on us and help us in making those decisions if we have predetermined the principles upon which our decisions will hinge. Those principles have to do with such simple matters as honesty and integrity, the importance one places on self-respect, and the scale of values by which one lives. Those matters need to be decided in advance if you plan to handle the crossroads where the signposts are down.

The third essential for living in a pressurized world is a faith in the usefulness of one's life. One of the great spirits of our day is a man in Princeton, New Jersey, named Ernest Gordon. Gordon has become nationally known as a minister and as an author. With his life, his words, and his books, he is speaking in a meaningful way to people everywhere.

During the Second World War, Gordon was an officer in the British infantry. After the fall of Sumatra, he attempted escape on a sailing vessel to Ceylon. He never made it. He was captured by the enemy.

Confined to the death camp on the River Kwai, Gordon was desperately ill. One medical officer said, "The only thing left is to let him have a decent end." One day another army doctor visited Gordon in his miserable little shack. "Ernest," he said, "we've been able to secure enough medicine on the black market to give you twelve shots. We need a thousand times that much. There are so many who need it."

"But why give it to me?" Gordon asked. "Give it to someone else. I'll make it."

"No go," said the doctor. "You will be dead in two weeks. Some of us think you can do something worthwhile with your life after this is over."

Gordon has written a book entitled *Meet Me at the Chapel Door*. In that book he tells the story of his life thus far. He says that he has been driven by the memory of those who believed he could do something that would really count.

Who knows what tomorrow's world will be like? We appear to be on the threshold of incredible discoveries. In a few years we may open heretofore uninhabitable parts of our globe. We may even visit distant planets. The possibilities of biological engineering may enable us to eliminate most pain, disease, and physical defects. We may even expand the limits of human life to unheard-of dimensions. But, whatever these circumstances may be, one thing appears certain: whether we live in a new world or an old one, there will still be an opportunity for a *single life* to do something meaningful —and for each person to find life worth living.

However, no one can function to his fullest potential until he has learned to cope with the pressures and frustrations that are inevitable in our kind of world. The chapters in this book are intended to help us consider some of the pressure points most of us are facing or will face in life. We will look for ways to handle these bewildering places. You are invited to take the journey. If you are out there in the storm, you may find a few signposts that will help you get through.

Something to Hold To

FINDING STABILITY IN A WORLD OF CHANGE

A radio station in one of our Southern cities recently aired a series of programs originally broadcast during pre-television days. The programs included such radio classics as "The Great Gildersleeve," "Fibber McGee and Molly," "Sam Spade," and "The Lone Ranger." The reaction in the city was interesting. A lot of television screens were blank as people turned on their radios. Young and old alike seemed to find the programs interesting.

In recent years a kind of nostalgia has been sweeping our land. Mickey Mouse watches, railroad pocket watches, bibbed overalls and the like have gained in popularity. Many specialists in human behavior believe this phenomenon reflects a dissatisfaction with contemporary life styles. There seems to be a deliberate effort to escape to "the good old days."

The trouble with this effort is that no one seems able to identify just when the good old days were. That is because there is a marked tendency among us to romanticize the past. The truth is that the good old days were not always good. A recent newspaper column described America 175 years ago. Life expectancy was thirty-eight years; the average work week was seventy-two hours; and the median annual wage was $300. On occasion, epidemics claimed the lives of entire families. Rivers carried cholera, typhoid, and yellow fever, and one of those diseases killed one out of five residents of Philadelphia in the year 1793. Most people don't know such grim facts. If they did, then those good old days might not seem so attractive. Yet the nostalgia wave continues. We'd like to get back to a world that was a little calmer and to a pace that was a bit slower.

However we look at it, the effort to recall the past reflects some distaste for the present. Modern people seem caught on a merry-go-round, and it moves with ever-increasing speed. Someone has said that present-day man is a sick fly on a spinning wheel. He is dizzy at the speed he travels. Before he can get adjusted to anything, it has been updated, revised, miniaturized, or made obsolete. There is a story about an error that appeared in a national newspaper. The error may have accidentally stated the truth. Quoting a well-known person on his reading habits, the editor intended to say, "I *read* three newspapers every day." The typesetter inadvertently hit an extra D. The sentence came out, "I *dread* three newspapers every day." Most of us feel this way, too, at times. We wonder what new crisis the newspaper or the television news will bring.

The question we ask is, "How can we keep our balance in a world of such incredible change?" A calendar published by an insurance firm a few years ago carried this slogan: "The way to endure change is to find something that never changes." There's a splendid thought in that sentence, but before we consider it we need to look for a moment at the way life actually goes.

Several years ago Alvin Toffler wrote a book that appeared on the best-seller lists for weeks. Toffler's thesis was that change feeds on itself and, in doing so, becomes an ever-tightening spiral. His projections for the next fifty years were frightening. He said that change will occur with devastating rapidity. Toffler may have overstated the case, but to some degree his observations were valid. We do live in a world of rapid change. Life is different today from what it was even in the immediate past. Things are not like they were, and they never will be again.

It is said that if Shakespeare came back today, he would recognize only five out of every nine words in the English language. The reason is simple: language is forever growing. New words are being added every year. The space-age vocabulary is different from that of the horse-and-buggy era, and computer language outdates that of typewriter days. In the 1950s we talked about cheap energy and we built our cars big and long. Twenty-five years later the "Rabbit" and other compact cars are being designed to conserve fuel. We are now told that the days of cheap energy are over. We can't even be certain of that, however. Who knows what new inventions lurk around the corner? The whole technical world is in a state of flux. A degree in engineering is said to be obsolete within five years after it is granted, unless some effort is made to update it.

What happens in the technical world also happens at other levels. Every individual finds change inevitable. The problems of childhood give way to those of youth. Those of youth yield to the difficul-

14

ties of being an adult. All of us confront these realities. There are the problems of parenthood and caring for aging parents. There are the uncertainties of health for ourselves and our loved ones. Death seems to know no justice or mercy: only rarely does it seem appropriate. And where is the person who doesn't spend some anxious moments worrying about a job or vocation? The river of life is a stream of change. It has always been that way.

It is this fact of change that forces us to seek something that is changeless. At a convocation of rural ministers recently, a young priest told about a little church in southern Texas. It had been built in the nineteenth century and had definitely seen better days. Every stone in its foundation had shifted. The steeple listed at least twenty degrees from center. The pulpit was so shaky it would hardly support the preacher. The young people of the congregation wanted to build a new church, but they met with stiff resistance. "We were married in that church," said some of the older members. "We want it to stay the same." The young priest said, "I longed to side with the supporters of the new church, but I didn't. I understood how the older people felt."

There is a basic need in all of us for something familiar and something that abides. That's true no matter what our age. A small child wants the same old tattered blanket or teddy bear, and the fairy tales read the same way every night. A youngster will exchange a party dress or suit for faded blue jeans or a worn-out jacket. We come home at night and look for an old pair of shoes. We feel comfortable with the familiar.

Have you ever been out on a winter evening when the sleet and snow became a raging blizzard? The wind howling with relentless fury, your steps turn homeward and suddenly the front door looms before you. There are the familiar smells of supper, the fire crackling in the fireplace, and the lamp burning by your favorite chair. How wonderful to relax in familiar surroundings where the unknowns are minimized. It is an age-old quest of people—this desire to feel at home.

The reasons for this quest have been evident for a long, long time. No one can stay out in the storm without some interval of rest and quiet. The human mind and body become exhausted and finally break down from too much stress. By the same token, to be forever with the familiar makes for boredom and monotony, which are equally deadly. Thus we need to alternate between change and the changeless. But we need not look for the changing—the world inevitably brings us that. What we do have to do is find our own places of refuge—the havens of the changeless.

16

How do we find such havens? One thing is certain: the answer is not geographical. Thomas Wolfe was right when he wrote *You Can't Go Home Again.* The people in that Texas congregation who wanted to preserve their church as it was were holding to a futile dream. Time dismantles even the sturdiest structures, and inexorably the old will be replaced with the new. Every security blanket eventually wears out, and the faded jeans become too tattered to wear. The persistent movement of the clock bears away the familiar faces of home. No place ever stays as it was. And the reason we can't go home again is that home isn't there any more.

Security is not a matter of geography but a condition of the mind and heart. It's not where we are that gives us stability in a changing world, but what we believe. There is an old story about a mountain man who lived in eastern Tennessee. For years his life had gone along as it had for the people of a century before. Then one day the rest of the world began to discover the beauty of his beloved hills. Roads were built through valleys and coves almost overnight. Power lines snaked across mountain peaks. His quiet world became a roaring tourist town. Through it all the old man remained calm and serene. A news reporter came by one day to interview the "natives." Impressed by the old man's placid spirit, the reporter asked the mountaineer if he was disturbed by all that was happening to him. "Shucks, no!" drawled the old-timer. "Ain't nothing going to happen that me and God together can't handle." That observation describes the secret of serene living in a world of change.

The person who holds himself together when the world is flying apart is the person who has an abiding conviction about who is really running the world. If it belonged solely to us, then there would be some reason for concern. Men and women in their restless quest for more and more of everything could well blow this planet to bits. There are those who believe that we do not have the final word on what happens to our world. Underneath what seems to be the trend toward destiny, these people observe an "unseen hand" at work. They believe that this "hand" is working toward a certain purpose and will use even our evil designs in achieving that purpose. These are the only people who can walk in the storm with peace in their hearts. The question, then, all of us need to ask if we intend to survive in this world of change, is, "What do I really believe about that unseen hand?"

The Time to Cross
a River
LEARNING TO CHOOSE

TWENTY-SIX miles out of Sylva, North Carolina, there is a spot known as the crest of the Blue Ridge Mountains. Here, the eastern half of the American continent is divided by the misty and majestic peaks of a mountain chain said by many to be among the most beautiful in the world. As one approaches this dividing line, a small spring by the side of the road can be seen. The water trickles forth and forms a sparkling little stream which makes its way down the lush green hills. For ten miles along that stream, one can cross it in a single step. However, somewhere down in the valley, the little stream is joined by another brook and becomes the Tuckasegee River. The Tuckasegee travels a turbulent channel and merges with such rivers as the Oconaluftee and the Nantahala. The names of the rivers change as they are joined by other streams. After a while, the waters of that little brook meet the mighty Mississippi. As the Mississippi reaches the sea at New Orleans, the great ocean-going vessels of the world float on its vast waters.

Anyone observing that little mountain stream will be impressed by its beauty, especially in the late afternoon. The sun burning against the evening clouds sets them aflame. The reflection of those clouds can be seen in the tangled waters of the stream. Now and then one will find a quiet pool so clear that the whole sky is mirrored like a giant canvas painted by a celestial brush. Only the most insensitive spirit can view that scene and not be moved to pensive reflection. One thinks about the majesty of creation and the intricate design and care the Creator used in planning his world.

A few years back a camper spent the evening by that little stream. Letting his mind wander, he began to think about the long journey the waters of the brook made as they flowed toward the sea. He remembered that where the stream began he could cross it easily, often in one step. But, as the channel widened, getting to the other side required more effort. Far down the way where the Mississippi meets the Gulf of Mexico, crossing the river became quite a task indeed. A thought came to that camper: "The time to cross a river is before it gets too wide."

One of the most difficult tasks of life is making choices. No one ever escapes that responsibility, although often one wishes one could. Sometimes making up one's mind is easy, but other times it is not. We face the hard choices, and the issues are unclear. We keep saying to ourselves, "If only I didn't have to decide." We learn, however, as all people before us have learned, that we *must* choose. At such a time, the thought of that mountain camper becomes crucial. "The time to cross a river is before to gets too wide." Several things are apparent in that thought.

First, think of this: there are moments in life when directions can be easily changed. Some four thousand years ago there were two shepherds caring for their sheep in a far-off land. The two men worked as brothers for a while, but one day there was trouble between them. They had a conference and finally one said to the other, "Let there be no strife between us. You decide which part of the land you want, and I'll take the other part." The shepherd surveyed the horizon. In the distance he saw that special part of the countryside where the grass grew tall and water was everywhere. "I'll go that way," he said selfishly. And off he went.

Down there in the direction the selfish shepherd chose was a city called Sodom. It was one of the toughest places on earth to live. No one who cared for the safety of his life and possessions ever went there. The selfish shepherd never intended to get to Sodom. He just wanted to go in that direction. Once he started, however, he couldn't turn back. We have the record of what happened. The shepherd did end up in that city and finally lost everything.

We need to remember that shepherd as we make our decisions. When we choose our directions, for a while at least, it's easy to turn back. That long-ago shepherd could have missed Sodom, but he kept going until the city reached out and devoured him. The brook gradually widens until it's difficult to cross.

There is a story about a tourist who stopped in a Southern town. He asked an old farmer, "Does it make any difference which road I take?" The old-timer thought for a moment and grunted, "Not to me, it don't!" From the farmer's point of view, it probably made no difference. But when you are the traveler, and the journey is life, it does! Different roads lead to different places. It's easy to turn back before you get too far. You can cross a river with little effort if it's not too wide.

This fact is especially significant for young people. Standing on the threshold of life, perhaps at graduation time, young people are confronted with countless open roads . . . so many possible directions. The consequences of a choice at this point are serious, but at least for a time it's easy to turn back and take a new road. Again, it's like that tiny mountain stream before it becomes a river: you can easily step to the other side.

James Russell Lowell had a somber thought when he wrote, in "Once to Every Man and Nation":

> Once to every man and nation
> Comes the moment to decide,
> In the strife of truth with falsehood,
> For the good or evil side;
> Some great cause, God's new Messiah,
> Offering each the bloom or blight,
> And the choice goes by forever
> Twixt that darkness and that light.

Lowell's thought is understandable. *Some* opportunities can be lost forever, but not *all* opportunities are forever lost. Life is hardly that rigid. You can always cross the river; but the earlier you cross it, the easier it is to get to the other side. This, in part, is the point of the proverb: "Don't make mountains out of molehills." Molehills don't need to become mountains if they are stopped in time.

Think of how little things become established patterns. There is in baseball something called "the seventh-inning stretch." According to an article in *Executive Digest,* that practice began when President Taft was watching a ballgame in Washington. Just after the seventh inning, he stood up to get the kinks out of his knees. The fans, thinking he was leaving, stood in respect. But the President sat down again and watched the rest of the game. Today, the seventh-inning stretch is as much a part of baseball as helping the umpire and scrambling for foul balls.

The principle here is a serious one in every area of life. We get hooked on status symbols, thought patterns, and putting off until tomorrow the things we should do today. Even in our businesses we sometimes hang on long after changes should be made: we try to work with yesterday's tools and hope to be in business tomorrow. Our personal lives are susceptible to these fixed directions. We have good intentions to spend more time with our families, to take a bit more time to "smell the roses," or to visit old friends. Meanwhile, however, other patterns of life are repeated so often that they become established and our good intentions are never realized. Work becomes a mania, occasional practices become habits, and experimental methods become traditions. It happens because we go down the river too far. The principle of inertia takes over and directs our lives.

Here is another thought: The price of crossing the river gets higher as the river gets wider. There is nothing complicated or unexpected about this fact. A tiny stream can be crossed in a single step, but a river calls for huge structures of steel and concrete if you want to get to the other side.

An awareness of this should force us to consider the things in our lives that need to be changed. Perhaps we need to rethink our vocations. Are we doing in life what we should be doing? Not all of us can find work we enjoy, but many of us can—and the rest if us can find ways of doing our work in more effective and satisfying ways. Maybe there are life-patterns that should be reversed. Countless Americans are so caught up with status symbols that they never realize that the price of keeping pace goes up as the years go by. For some of us there is a need to rethink our priorities. We don't take enough time to see the flowers along the way. Our friendships fade; the fun we should be having with our families gets pushed aside by less important things. How easy it is to spend one's life on roads that go nowhere. An old prophet once asked, "Why spend your money for that which is not bread?" What he meant, of course, was that many pursuits in life bring no real satisfaction. And the farther you go, the more difficult it is to cross the river.

There is, however, one grand and glorious truth about life: no circumstance is hopeless. The river never gets so wide that some changes can't be made. We can't start over, but we can start from where we are. Perhaps we can't take a whole new direction, but at least tomorrow can be slightly different from today. Just as old patterns become fixed by repetition, new patterns can be adopted if we are willing to pay the price.

There is a story of a man who lived long ago. This man spent the early years of his life hunting down and executing people his government considered undesirables. He was both hated and feared by most of his contemporaries. One day on a desert journey he decided to "cross the river" and begin a new life. He did! It took a long time, but he finally made it to the other side, and few people have had a greater impact on history than St. Paul. Paul crossed the river when it was a mighty stream. Had he done it earlier, it would have been easier. The lesson of his life is a lesson to us all. If you need to take a new direction, the earlier you make that decision, the easier it will be. The time to cross a river is before it gets too wide.

26

It's All Right to Worry

WORRYING CONSTRUCTIVELY

M o s t Americans are acquainted with Erma Bombeck. Her syndicated columns and television appearances have had wide exposure across the land. Her gentle humor is always delightful and, like that of Will Rogers, usually makes a lot of sense. Not long ago one of her books was on the best-seller list for weeks. It had the charming title of *If Life Is a Bowl of Cherries, What Am I Doing in the Pits?* In the epilogue to that book, Mrs. Bombeck makes an interesting confession: "I am," she said, "an orthodox worrier."

Not many people would be candid enough to admit addiction to anxiety. It is interesting to note that the word *worry* is derived from an Old English word which means literally "to strangle." Most of us have had that sensation. In moments of mental confusion, or fear, or apprehension, we feel as if something had us by the throat. Worry, when it is intense, can be paralyzing. Our mental processes are blurred, our personalities are distorted, and our bodies are robbed of appetite and sleep.

While worry is not listed among the Mortal Sins, we nevertheless consider it incompatible with a well-adjusted life. There is, to be sure, some reason for this: many, if not most, of our worries are emotionally and perhaps physically destructive. And there is a lot to be said for taking life as it comes. Someone tells of a sign that appeared on a barbershop in a sleepy little town: "Closed on account of improved financial position. May reopen next week, but a lot depends on financial position then."

That may be a great way to live—doing only what you have to do and never being apprehensive over what's coming next. When any virtue is pressed too far, however, it can become evil. That's true with "just hanging loose." Halford Luccock once suggested that there should be a book reversing the key words of the title of the one-time best-seller *How to Stop Worrying and Start Living*.

Dr. Luccock's comment was not intended to negate the point of that best-seller on worry. He knew that worrying is both dangerous and futile. What Dr. Luccock had in mind was not to encourage worry; rather, he was warning us not to fall out of the boat on the other side. If it is a mistake to be too apprehensive about life, it is also a mistake to take life too lightly. There should be a way to ponder the affairs of life without running the risk of mental and emotional breakdown. The question is, how do we achieve that balance?

We need to start by remembering that there is a distinction between *worry* and *concern*. One day, Jesus walked out of a little town located on the banks of a beautiful lake. He took a position on a hill overlooking that lake and began talking to the people who had followed him. "Why be anxious?" he asked. "Consider the birds of the air—they neither sow nor gather into barns; and yet your heavenly Father feeds them. Are you not of more value than they? Or consider the lilies of the field, how they grow; they toil not, neither do they spin. Yet, Solomon in all his glory was not arrayed like one of these. O, ye of little faith!"

Here we have it—an instruction from the wisest man who ever lived, telling us not to worry. Yet, this same man on another occasion is pictured as being heartbroken over the forthcoming destruction of his beloved city, Jerusalem. He is reported as saying, "O, Jerusalem, Jerusalem, how often have I sought to help you, but you wouldn't let me." Here are two examples that seem to offer us contradictory instructions. How are we to make sense of them?

We must remember that the first instruction was an intended exaggeration. Birds do die of starvation, and the Creator neither feeds nor clothes us. Nature sometimes deals harshly with life. When we are left to the mercy of the elements, we can suffer unimaginable pain. An absolute and literal acceptance of the first instruction would be sheer folly. Creation does not condone laziness, indolence, or total indifference to living. The point of these two instructions is based on the distinction between worry and concern. On the one hand *worry* is a fruitless anxiety about life that never results in anything creative. *Concern*, on the other hand, is the constructive application of energy to worthwhile matters. Concern is not aimless apprehension over problems but the search for answers.

Many of us never really understand this difference between worry and concern. Consequently, we spend our time lamenting what has happened rather than asking what we can do about it now that it has happened. Worry strangles life. Concern makes life an exciting adventure. Worry races the engine needlessly. Concern harnesses energy and makes it productive. Worry places the emphasis on whether you win or lose, while concern has to do with how well you run the race.

There are two areas especially where wholesome concern is not only important but also necessary: First, we need to think about what we are as opposed to what we can be. A lot is being said these days about "self-acceptance." When properly understood, this attitude of mind is commendable. Many of us do not fully appreciate our own uniqueness. We are envious of other people—where they are, and what they have. That kind of thinking is futile. We can't fit ourselves into another's mold, and, if we could, we probably wouldn't like it when we saw the total picture. There is an old fable about a day when the citizens of Rome gathered at the Forum to exchange troubles. Each person threw his troubles into the fountain's pool and was then allowed to select the trouble that seemed to fit his circumstances best. To the surprise of all, each person took home the same troubles he brought. When we really know the truth about others, we are less likely to envy them.

We all have our troubles, limitations, and handicaps. On any given day they may differ in degree and kind. But those who really understand people soon discover that, behind the masks we wear, all

of us have about all we can carry. The wisest decision we can make, therefore, is to accept ourselves
and go from there.

We need to remember, however, that self-acceptance is not the same as self-satisfaction. It's one
thing to accept where we are; it's a different matter
entirely to be content just to stay there. Arthur J.
Moore, a widely known churchman, used to tell
about a young minister who asked his bishop to hold
a quiet hour in the young minister's church. The
bishop responded, "What your church needs is not
a quiet hour but an earthquake. I don't want to be
as quiet as some of your people until I'm dead."
That's pretty blunt, but maybe it needed to be. For
all of us there is a difference between the *achieved*
self and the *potential* self.

This difference is a valid area for concern, and we
should be troubled about it. It's only when we are
dissatisfied with what we are that we strive to become what we can be. The people who have made
the greatest contribution to our lives are those who
"stir us up" and give us a vision of greater potential.
Perhaps it was a teacher who returned a paper with
the note, "You can do better than this," or a boss
who said the same thing. We owe a lot to people
who won't let us rest, who keep us concerned about
being better and doing better.

The second area where concern is necessary is about the difference between our actual world as opposed to our possible world. Several years ago a United States senator gave an address at his brother's funeral. Edward Kennedy made this arresting comment: "I've heard my brother say many times, 'Some men see things as they are and say why. I dream things that never were and say why not!'" We owe our civilization (to the degree we are civilized) to those who ask, "Why not?"

Isn't all progress the result of someone's dissatisfaction? The wheel was invented by someone who became tired of dragging or carrying heavy loads. We live in warm houses, eat cooked food, have hospitals to care for the sick and schools to educate our children, all because someone was not comfortable with the way things were. If we solve our energy problems, clean up our environment, and build a world of peace, these things will come about because someone was dissatisfied. We need to be concerned about such things.

It is said that Abraham Lincoln once saw a slave being sold at an auction and realized how inhuman such a system was. He declared, "If I ever get a chance, I'll hit slavery hard." He didn't rest until he had made for himself a chance to hit it. The debt the world owes to dissatisfied people is worth think-

33

ing about. Suppose no one had ever cared and no one had ever been concerned. What would our world be like?

Now let's move this principle down to a more intimate and personal level. We may not be able to help being where we now find ourselves, but we can decide what we are going to do about it. There is an old prayer widely quoted: "Lord, give me the grace to accept what I can't change, the courage to change the things I can change, and the wisdom to know the difference." That's a lovely thought, but it is also mostly untrue. The fact is we can do something about everything. If nothing else, we can change our attitude toward it. We may have a handicap that is medically beyond correction. We can't change that; but if we are concerned enough and thoughtful enough, we can find a way to use that handicap.

A long time ago a man was imprisoned in a Roman jail. He wrote a sentence which has been widely misunderstood: "I have learned that in whatever circumstance I find myself, therewith to be content." If you think this man had settled in and given up, you are wrong. He did accept the fact that he was in jail, but he did not give up. He used his time to write letters, and those letters finally became the major portion of the world's most important book, the New Testament. St. Paul had found the secret to adventurous living. He did something about everything, and he used whatever happened to him.

Are you an "orthodox worrier?" Why not be an "unorthodox" one? It requires no more effort, and it's far more healthy and productive. The next time you are restless, "up tight," spending a sleepless night, try a new approach. Don't spend precious time in self-pity, running over what has happened. Just ask the question, "Now that this has happened, what can I do about it?" If you look long and carefully, you will discover at least one direction in which you may go. You will be surprised how your world and life can become different. Indeed, it's all right if you "worry" this way.

You Don't Miss It Until It's Gone

LEARNING TO LIVE IN THE PRESENT

T H E R E is a little publication that makes the rounds among the employees of a Southern school system. The publication is designed to acquaint teachers with study guides, announcements of up- coming events, and the latest news about the teach- ing profession. The last page of the paper is entitled "Small Wit and Wee Wisdom." Here teachers re- late their experiences in teaching America's youth.

Now and then the teachers report on some of the papers they receive from their students. Recently one teacher told of a word–meaning test given some third-grade pupils. A list of words was mimeographed, and the children were asked to supply definitions. Some of the answers were serious; others were humorous. One teacher asked her children to define the word "salt." A third-grader came up with an interesting thought: "Salt is what you don't notice until someone forgets to put it in."

Whether or not that definition originated with that youngster is problematical, but it suggests something that has profound implications for life. We take a lot of things for granted in our world until, for some reason, they are absent. Back in the military history of an ancient people, there is an old story about a soldier who was given a prisoner to guard. Apparently, holding the prisoner was of crucial importance because the instructions to the soldier were specific: "Guard this prisoner at all costs. If he escapes, you will forfeit your life." We don't know exactly what happened, but the record states that when the soldier was finally called to present his prisoner, the prisoner had fled. The soldier gave this excuse: "As I was busy here and there, the prisoner was gone." There is something truly pathetic about that soldier's confession. Bind it together with the schoolboy's definition of salt, and you come up with some important ideas.

Begin by remembering that we never miss so many things that are vital to us until they are gone.

37

In the want-ad section of a recent American newspaper, there was a curious little sentence: "Dear Jane, I love you more than duck-hunting." It was signed, "Bill." No one knows why that ad appeared in the newspaper. One suspects that it came about as a result of a domestic quarrel. There may have been an argument over Bill's spending too much time away from home, and Jane may have issued an ultimatum. Perhaps her husband, completely angry, had refused to accept Jane's decision and so Jane left. However, when heated emotions cooled, perhaps Bill had made a discovery: that what he had lost was far more important than he had dreamed.

That's a perfectly human discovery, and a lot of us make it. In one of America's most popular television programs, "All in the Family," the program begins with the Bunkers singing, "Those Were the Days." The words of that song seem to reflect a kind of nostalgia for days long past—days that were filled with good things that will never be again.

It is not at all unusual for us to project the good days into the past or the future. Elsewhere in this book we have considered our tendency to romanticize the past. We also romanticize the future. Listen to the dreams of people you meet almost every day. The young person looks forward with anticipation to graduation as a day when the discipline of school is no more. The mother will long for the time when her children are grown and married, because she will then be free of the countless tasks that tie her to the home. Business people think about their next promotion, imagining themselves to be rid of the monotony of their present job. An older person longs for that grand day of retirement when he is free to make his own schedule and plan his own agenda. But observe how often we look back on life and, in retrospect, discover that what we thought to be the hard times now seem to be the good times. A lot of young people later reflect on their school days and long for the carefree times spent as a student. The mother will sit at her child's wedding and remember the times she and her children played lovingly together. Retired people, after a few weeks of relaxation, reflect on the days when their work was exciting and challenging. "Those were the days," we say. For so many people, the happy times always seem to be in the future or the past. We find it difficult to appreciate the present.

Someone has rightly said that if the stars could be seen only one night a year, everyone would see them. As it is, many people never see them. This same principle carries over into more strategic areas in our lives. Few people really appreciated clean air and pure water until they became polluted by our careless wastefulness. Few of us really appreciate our families as we should until we are deprived of their presence by death or extended separation. The real value of a friend is not recognized until that friend is gone. That third-grade student had unwittingly touched on a lot of things when he suggested that salt is what you don't notice until someone forgets to put it in. It's true of friendship, health, meaningful work, families, and a host of other important blessings. We never miss them until they are gone.

There is a second idea worth remembering. Sometimes we become preoccupied with lesser things to the point where important things are lost. A few years ago a speaker at a college commencement made an address with an intriguing title: "Things I Know for Certain." He referred to the constant motion of the human situation and pointed out that ideas once considered absolute are now giving way to new discoveries. Newtonian physics is adjusted by Einstein's discoveries. Historical mysteries are unraveled by new archeological research. "But," said the speaker, "some things seem to remain inflexible even in a world of change. One of them is this: Life is short."

There are those who would take issue with that thought. At times all of us feel that time moves at a snail's pace. It's seldom that way, however, when time is viewed in retrospect. A conversation with older people offers evidence of this. "It seems as if it were only yesterday," they say, "when our children were small. How quickly they grow up and are gone." Or, "I can't believe so many years have gone by since that event happened." The structure of life is such that, the older we get, the more rapidly the years seem to go by. For a child, Christmas is an eternity away. For older people, the bills of one Christmas are scarcely paid before they are confronted with bills for the next one.

That commencement speaker was right. Life does slip away. It's sobering how many literary descriptions of life deal with its brevity. Someone has said that life is like a flower: it springs up in the morning and withers in the evening. Another said that life is like the mist which the morning sun drives away. Still another writer declared that living is as a tale which is soon told. Life *is* short; and while we are busy, here and there, it gets away.

Christopher Morley wrote a poem entitled "End of August." When you read it, you get the picture of a person who takes time for granted. There are a lot of things to do, but they do not seem pressing. The person muses contentedly. Then comes a final line in the poem which rings with startling reality: "Chattering voltage like a broken wire/The wild cicada cried, Six weeks to frost!"

No thoughtful person can read those lines without somber reflection. Life does have a point of termination, and we won't pass this way again. It's so easy to squander precious days, postponing happiness to the future or wasting the present living in the past. There is a crude but impressive phrase often heard among young people, "Don't sweat the small stuff." Older people could well heed the truth of that. While you are busy here and there, life does get away. It's tragic to waste it on trivial things—things that in the long run simply do not matter.

All of this suggests a final thought. It has to do with the importance of the "now" life. A few years ago, Mae West was reflecting on her life. The reporter conducting the interview asked her what she would do differently if she could live again. Her answer came after a long moment of thought: "If I could live again, I would try to appreciate good things before I lost them."

That's a worthy resolution and is echoed so often by so many thoughtful people. In the spring of 1913, Sir William Osler made an address at Yale University entitled, "A Way of Life." This was his theme: "Live neither in the past nor in the future, but let each day's work absorb all your interest, energy, and enthusiasm. The best preparation for tomorrow is to do today's work superbly well."

William Hale White once wrote, "As I got older I became aware of the folly of this perpetual reaching after the future and of drawing from tomorrow and tomorrow only, a reason for the joyfulness of today. I learned, when alas! it was almost too late, to live each moment as it passed over my head."

Arnold Bennett wrote a book which became a classic in its time. He called it *How to Live on Twenty-Four Hours a Day*. One idea from that book still makes the rounds: "You wake up in the morning and lo, your purse is magically filled with twenty-four hours. It is yours. It is the most precious of possessions. Its most effective use is the matter of highest urgency." That's the point of those famed lines from Omar Khayyám:

> Tomorrow's fate, though thou be wise,
> Thou canst not tell nor yet surmise;
> Pass, therefore, not today in vain,
> For it will never come again.

These words should speak to us in a world where living seems to be a constant mad dash. Howard Murray in his book *Salt O' Life* told a story about an old mountaineer who offered a friend some sage advice. The friend came by to visit and appeared to be in a great rush. "Hurry?" asked the mountain man. "Why, don't you know a man will overrun a heap more'n he'll ever overtake?" That's a quaint way of suggesting that it's possible to miss the best things as we go along and never find the good days we so relentlessly pursued.

Life needs to be lived in the "now." It takes only a moment to feel the freshness of a crisp morning or to glance at a tree laden with the crystals of new fallen snow. A moment spent gazing at a sunset can put new sparkle in your life. An evening by the fireside with family and friends, who so often want something more than money can buy, can be an unforgettable experience. It isn't how much time you take to "smell the roses"; it's how you use the time you have. But never let a day pass without finding a moment of joy.

If you have been missing life as you go along, you may well miss it altogether. Happiness is not over the next hill or down the road. It can be found *now*. Many of us are passing by what we are really trying to find. The uncertainties of life press the question upon us. If you have your health, enjoy it while you have it. If you have a family, take some time with them while they are still around. If there is a bit of beauty nearby, pause a moment to enjoy it. Start living *now*. It may be all the living you will have time to do.

Nibbled by the Minnows

BATTLING CRITICISM

O N a November day in 1863, the citizens of Gettysburg, Pennsylvania, held a special memorial observance that will long be remembered in American history. Invited to address the gathering were the president of the United States and a widely-known senator from Massachusetts named Edward Everett. Everett preceded the president on the platform. He spoke for an hour and fifty-seven minutes. His address was so eloquent that the crowd cheered with wild enthusiasm. When the senator had finished, the president was introduced. He read a 267-word speech and took his seat.

45

The following morning, newspapers across the land carried the report of the Gettysburg observance. In most of the papers, Everett was acclaimed as one of America's finest orators. The president, however, was treated far less kindly. One editorial writer was reported to have said, "The president is a cunning clown. He is the original gorilla. Those who seek the ape are fools to go to Africa when he can be found in the White House in Washington." Today the world has a different estimate of those two speakers on that long-ago day in Gettysburg. Few Americans remember the senator's speech, but almost every school child can quote from Lincoln's address.

Seldom has anyone been more severely censured and criticized than was Lincoln in his day. It is true, of course, that not many of us make it through this world without being subjected to the harsh judgment of others. Recently the editor of one of America's popular magazines declared, "I don't like criticism—constructive or otherwise—but we are getting it more than ever these days. I am being forced to adopt some wholesome attitudes toward it, for it is the most valuable service our readers can render." That editor was making a worthy resolution. The constructive use of even destructive criticism is a marvelous achievement. The question is: how do we manage to use it?

46

The first thing we must learn in using criticism constructively is to expect it. In one of the oldest books in the world, there is a little verse that reads, "Judge not, lest you be judged." If the point of that instruction is to prohibit an evaluation of people, it is obviously impossible. Every time we cast a ballot, embark on a business venture, choose an employer or employee, buy a used car or even a bag of groceries, we sit in judgment on someone or something. Our critical faculties are essential to our social existence, and our failure to exercise those faculties can be devastating. At the same time most of us expect to be subjected to critical examination by others when the reasons are good and valid.

There are judgments, however, that are unnecessary and not nearly so wholesome. Years ago in a little booklet there was a sentence that is descriptive of human nature. "Mediocrity has a way of resenting excellence." Whoever wrote that sentence was fully aware of our chronic temptation to minimize our own imperfections by maximizing the faults of others. That kind of criticism is the oldest strategy in the world—the attempt to build ourselves up by pulling others down.

Anyone who has been out in the world for any period of time knows about this method of attack. He will be especially aware of it if he attempts to be a front-runner. Lift your head above the crowd, and you become a target. The reason is that it's easier to ridicule than to compete. Every person who achieves excellence, whether in his vocation or his avocation, needs to remember this. Excellence inevitably breeds its own resistance. If we expect to live above the level of mediocrity, the thickness of our armor must increase in proportion to our chosen altitude. The failure to remember this leads to troubled times. No one hits the top without feeling the hounds of jealousy and envy nipping at heels. If it is any consolation, it helps to know that the critic often reveals more about himself than the object of his criticism. It's the little people who nibble at the lives of the great.

It's not enough, of course, simply to expect criticism when you walk the high road. We must pursue a second principle. If harsh judgment is to serve any good purpose, we must learn from it. A lot of stories have been circulated about Abraham Lincoln. Whether they are fact or legend does not diminish their lessons. You may recall that one of the members of Lincoln's cabinet once called the president a fool. Lincoln replied, "Well, Stanton is a wise man; if he called me a fool, I had better look into it." If that story is true, then one can easily understand Lincoln's greatness.

This is not to suggest that criticism does not hurt. It does, as anyone who has been subjected to it fully understands. Criticism is often inspired by prejudices. We can be the victims of racism, sexism, social or religious bigotry. In such a framework judgments against us become distorted and malicious. We are usually upset and angry when we are the targets of such vicious abuse and we have every right to be. But it is a wise person indeed who searches through even the most unjust criticism for any element of truth. If some fault is found, we must not allow our resentment to blind us to it. The best way to get even with unfair critics is to learn from them.

The truth is that only through the testing fires of criticism do we grow. It is a foolish leader who surrounds himself with "yes" men. I remember a man many years ago who said that everyone should have at least two friends: one who agrees with him and another who does not. They are equally valuable. The friend who is agreeable and supportive will enable us to maintain our balance, and the other friend will keep us from becoming complacent. Those words of wisdom are ignored at great peril. Often it is in the shock of the harsh blast of criticism that we learn most about ourselves.

Now and then in professional schools, students are offered courses in public speaking. One of the exercises usually involved in such courses is the preparation and delivery of a speech for fellow stu-

49

dents. The role of the class is to analyze the speech with the most critical judgment. Those who have undergone such an exercise find it an ego-shattering experience. But when they review that day from some distant vantage point, most will admit that it was their most profitable training.

It is said that Thomas Edison was often interrupted by well-wishers who came to visit him out of curiosity. Edison found many such visits frustrating and of little value. But his ingenuity found a way to turn those seemingly useless visits into a profit. He attached a pump to the gate, so that every visitor who came through pumped water into a reservoir. That's a marvelous way to come at life—using everything that happens to you for something good. The painful barbs of criticism should not be excluded from that list. The truth is that we sometimes learn more about ourselves from our enemies than we do from our friends.

There is a third step in acquiring a positive attitude toward criticism. While we may learn from our critics, we must never allow their criticisms to deflect us from holding to a matter of conscience or pursuing a worthy goal. Down in the Deep South many years ago, there was an eccentric minister who had his own quaint way of stating ideas. One of his favorite expressions was, "I don't mind being swallowed by a whale, but I'm not going to be nibbled to death by the minnows." This was his way of saying that, if you are going to lose, then lose in a great battle with a worthy foe. Never allow your defeat to result from the nibbles of minor opponents.

One of Aesop's fables is about a man and his son who were leading a donkey to town. A passerby laughed at them for walking while the donkey had no load, so the man had the boy ride. Before long they met a man who took the boy to task for riding while his poor, tired father walked. The boy got off the donkey, and the man got on. Soon another traveler called the man selfish because he was making the little boy walk. To neutralize this objection they both got on the donkey, only to be accused of cruelty to the animal. In desperation they tied the donkey's feet together, put a pole between them, and began to carry the donkey. But people laughed so much that they let the donkey down. As they did, the animal began to kick and rolled into the river and drowned. There is no need to state the moral of that story—it's perfectly clear.

Hugh Latimer, the famed English cleric, was once invited to speak before the king of England. As he was preparing for the appearance, he said, "I heard an inner voice saying, 'Latimer, be careful what you say today because you will speak before the king.' But after a while," he said, "I heard another voice saying, 'Latimer, be careful what you say today because you will be speaking before the King of Kings.' "

We all stand in a higher court than the one where we are judged by our fellow man. It is the verdict of that higher court that really counts. The secret to great living is to have a clear conscience no matter what the judgment of our detractors may be. When you learn to live at that level, you can listen to the nibblers, learn from them, and still be at peace.

Are You Tired?

HANDLING WEARINESS

I t ' s been reprinted thousands of times—that lovely little picture of a boy carrying a much younger lad. The artist, whoever he was, managed to convey the impression that the older boy is struggling under a heavy load. As the boy lugs the younger lad along, someone must have asked him a question, for underneath the picture there is this line: "He ain't heavy; he's my brother." Somehow this portrait catches our interest. You can see it posted in offices and homes and printed in magazines and periodicals. A few years ago someone wrote a song about it, and it was sung everywhere. The title was, as you would expect, "He Ain't Heavy; He's My Brother."

There are a lot of lessons in that little picture, and one of the most important has to do with the way in which our thought processes influence our physical endurance. We live in a world where the pace is relentless and intense. While there are some people who do not feel the pressure and for whom the days skip by in a leisurely way, most of us are not able to enjoy the luxury of taking our time. We feel driven and pursued by clocks and calendars with never enough time to do everything that needs to be done. It was Julia Ward Howe, the famed author of the "Battle Hymn of the Republic," who once said: "I'm tired way down into the future." A housewife picking up on that thought whimsically declared, "I'm so far behind that if anything else were to happen, it would be at least two weeks before I could worry about it."

Most of us, when we are in this predicament, imagine we are having a harder time of it than others have had. In many ways it is true that the complexities of our day keep us under greater pressure than they did in the days of our predecessors. But our age has no corner on busy people. Twenty centuries ago a man wrote a letter to some friends in which he penned an interesting line: "Let us not be weary in well-doing, for in due season we shall reap if we faint not." One would conclude from this exhortation that even then there were people who knew what it meant to carry heavy loads. Often they were tempted to turn back. But this long-ago writer is saying to his friends, "Don't give up and throw in the towel." The people who read this ancient letter must have asked the same question we ask: "How can we carry on?"

Of course, a part of our weariness results from sheer physical exhaustion, and the only answer to that is rest. But that isn't all of the answer. A part of our lack of endurance is related to the way we think. Some of our weariness, for instance, has to do with our sense of purpose.

About a hundred years ago, Friedrich Nietzsche, the renowned philosopher, did some writing which many believe became the blueprint for modern Nazism. If that is true, then Nietzsche brought the world an inestimable tragedy. But even in his sometimes perverted and twisted thinking this philosopher said some things worth remembering. On one occasion he declared that we could endure the "how" of any circumstance if we could but understand the "why." Years later, in our present world, we have come to understand the sense of that. The knowledge of purpose has bearing on our endurance. More often than we imagine, our stamina is lost because we lose our goals and objectives.

One of the quaint stories coming out of southern Appalachia is about a farmer who found it difficult to travel from one place to another because he was always getting lost. One day he was asked about his problem. He declared that as a boy he had learned to read "figurin'" but not "writin'." As a result, he said, when he saw a road sign he could tell "how fur" but never "where to." That's a widespread problem when stated in a slightly different way. A lot of us are running, but we don't know why or where. That always makes the race wearisome. This could well be implied in the picture of the boy who was carrying his brother. The little fellow may have been hurt, and the older brother was trying to get him home. That very purpose gave wings to the boy's feet. It's always easier to run when you understand the reason.

Any mother can understand this. Hospital waiting rooms are filled with those who keep a silent vigil, sometimes for days on end. Down the hall a child is sick. The doctor will encourage the mother to go home, but the mother insists she isn't tired. In a very real sense she is telling the truth. A mother's endurance is almost limitless when her child's life is in danger. Nietzsche was right. You can endure almost any circumstance if you understand the purpose.

Industry has long since been aware of this. Workers on an assembly line whose jobs involve the most monotonous tasks become far more efficient when they know how their simple tasks fit into the end result. Billy Graham tells somewhere about a stone worker who was given an order for some strangely designed carvings. He worked with little enthusiasm. Finally one day when his work was completed, he was invited to the site where his carvings were being used. When he saw how his work fitted into the lovely design of a great building, he declared: "My hand would have been steadier and my work easier if I had known why I was working." That's the way it usually happens. People who have a purpose find it easier to run and not get weary.

Perhaps a part of the reason for the weariness of our times is the loss of a sense of meaning for our lives. We are caught up in a maze of ill-defined goals and drive ourselves to distraction over things that do not matter. The happy people are those who know *why* they are busy. They are running for a reason that counts.

Another cause for our weariness is related to the feeling of loneliness. People who engage in mountain climbing seldom practice their sport alone. There are many reasons, not the least of which is safety. Another hand on the rope can mean the difference between life and death when you are struggling against the face of a treacherous ledge. But every climber toiling against height, wind, and storm recognizes the importance of having a comrade in the spirit of the journey. It's a lot easier to keep going if someone is nearby to urge you on.

There is a marvelous story in the Bible about a man who was trying to stand for the "best of things in the worst of times." As often happens when someone attempts a great cause, there was opposition. One day this man was challenged. His life was threatened, and he was frightened into despair. Retreating to a faraway place of safety, he almost surrendered to suicide. But out there in the desert, he heard a voice. "Elijah, you are not alone. There are seven thousand people back home who are willing to stand by your side." Elijah arose and went back to his task with renewed vigor. It makes a difference in the way you run when you know you aren't running alone. The people who accomplish incredible things against impossible odds are the people who sense someone nearby. Sometimes that "someone" is a visible person; at other times, it's an "unseen runner" who travels by your side.

We have known it for a long time: people working together can accomplish more than the sum total of those same people working alone. There is a contagious enthusiasm in numbers that gives added endurance to each individual involved. Thus it's a wise person, indeed, who shares his race with a friend. Find someone either in body or in spirit to run with you, and the race is easier to run.

Finally, weariness is related to our sense of hope. Halford Luccock tells about a village in the hills of New England doomed to extinction by a proposed power dam. When word of the dam spread through the town, the people were demoralized. All building stopped and every improvement came to a standstill. The town was soon dilapidated and ghostly. Someone reporting the spirit of the people declared, "Where there is no faith in the future, there is no power in the pursuit."

That's the way it goes. People grow weary in a hurry when they see no hope of winning. Karl Menninger tells about a group of doctors who survived the horrors of slave labor in a World War II concentration camp. Each night they secretly came together and shared their knowledge in a small medical society. They believed that someday what they were learning and sharing would be of benefit to the world. "Kept alive by *hope*" was the reason given for their survival.

You have heard it said again and again: "My faith sustained me. Without it, I could not have carried on." These are not just idle or meaningless words. Rather, they suggest a truth as eternal as the ages. When you believe in what you are doing—that somewhere, sometime, you can win—you can run and not be weary.

We are tired people in a tired world. We feel harassed and pressured. A part of our problem is physical. We drive our bodies beyond their design and carry loads we can never handle without proper rest. But for many of us the problem is spiritual and emotional. We haven't really searched for and found a purpose for living. We attempt to battle life all alone without a seen or an unseen friend. Even more damaging is the effort to run without an inner faith that life can be victorious, if not in one way then in another. The results are weary bodies, troubled minds, and restless hearts.

That old picture is worth thinking about—"He ain't heavy; he's my brother." When you have a reason to run, someone to run with you, and faith in a victory somewhere, it's amazing how quickly you can find your "second wind."

What's the Use?

ESCAPING FUTILITY

S E V E R A L years ago Lowell Russell Ditzen told of sitting with a man at a banquet in New York City. The man held a distinguished place in the business community and had dealt with intricate legal and economic problems. During the evening the man said, "I have to answer the most difficult letter I have ever received. It came two days ago from my son, who is a sophomore in college. In substance it said, 'Dad, why should I dig into literature, the physical sciences, and sociology when it looks like I shall be pulled into the army and will probably spend the most important years of my life in a war? The fellows here are discouraged. There doesn't seem to be much chance for a normal life for us. Some are saying, "Why try to do our best when the world is going to hell?" ' "

Dr. Ditzen told of this experience in a sermon preached in Bronxville, New York, in 1950. Nearly thirty years have passed since that question was raised by the troubled college student. During those years the world has bounced about from the brink of one disaster to another. At times it has seemed that the end was in sight. The world, however, appears to be made of pretty resilient stuff. In many ways it is a better world. We have made great strides in conquering disease and alleviating pain. We are taking more seriously some of the gigantic problems confronting us. We are attempting to deal with grave environmental problems which our carelessness has produced. We are making more effort to talk about our international problems instead of fighting over them. We know about the dreadful plight of hungry people, and there seems to be a new conscience among affluent people to aid them. Still, there is much evidence suggesting that the world is yet a dangerous place. We haven't eliminated war, solved the food problem, or abolished crime. In the face of such immense problems, the question suggested by a college student thirty years ago lingers. A lot of people wonder why they should do their best when so many things seem hopeless.

One factor complicates this problem even more. The overwhelming number of us on this planet seems to minimize the unique importance of the individual. There is a lot of complaining about the depersonalization of people. We feel as if we are insignificant cogs in a giant cosmic wheel. Business looks upon us as consumers. The people in professional vocations think of us as clients. Medicine has made us patients, and computer science has made us into numbers. Even government, which ideally is supposed to serve us, has somehow come to see us as the servants of the state. It is not surprising that so many of us have feelings of uselessness and futility. We really wonder why we should keep on trying when the world is going to hell.

The problem that arises is how do we answer the question. It isn't likely that a few words in a brief chapter of a book can speak in depth to the matter. It is possible, however, that a few ideas can open areas of thought.

Anyone who is troubled with a sense of futility, for instance, might well spend some time thinking about the nature of our world. If anything is evident in creation, it is that we live in a still-developing society. Civilization is still in its infancy. Several years ago someone came up with a striking parable. The reference was to Cleopatra's Needle, which stands on the banks of the River Thames in London. He said that if a penny were placed on the top of the monument and a postage stamp on the penny, the following comparison could be made: the pillar would represent the time the earth has been in existence; the penny, the length of man's existence on earth; and the postage stamp the length of time man has been civilized. Or, to put it another way, if we reduced to the scale of a single year the total time life has been on this planet, man stood upright on the afternoon of December 31. At two minutes before the end of that year, Christ appeared on our planet.

Sometimes I think it helps to take a look at where we stand on the scale of time. We often refer to the long struggle of man up the hill of civilization, when in reality the process has just begun. If that is true, then it is unlikely that we should reach utopia in so short a time. There is nothing anywhere to guarantee that by this year in the twentieth century the earth would be a paradise.

Every generation has been up against a world full of problems, and never have the people in any age been able to lead a "normal" life. Back in 170 B.C., Antiochus the Great was on his way home from Egypt where he had been rebuffed by the Romans.

Mad with rage, he decided to vent his anger on the city of Jerusalem. He attacked the city and took it almost without effort. It is said that eighty thousand inhabitants of the city were killed and ten thousand were sold into slavery. Antiochus sacked the temple in the city, turned it into a Greek shrine, and forbade the people to worship their God. Those found in defiance of his orders were brutally tormented and finally killed. Seldom in history has there been a more sadistic and deliberate attempt to annihilate a people and their culture.

What do you suppose a son asked his father when he wrote home from Jerusalem in those days? Do you imagine that he was concerned about the worthiness of his efforts—whether there was any reason to do his best when his world was going up in smoke? Or what about the people who lived through the Black Death epidemic in Europe, when it is estimated that from one-fourth to three-fourths of the continent's population was wiped out? When all of history is brought into focus, one wonders if "what's the use?" is not the perennial question of *all* people. This, of course, does not solve our problem, but it helps to know that we are not the first people to confront it.

Another thing that helps in handling the sense of futility is this: of the two alternatives open to us—struggle or surrender—only struggle gives meaning to life. There are only two things that any of us can do about our world. One of them is to throw in the towel and let the world go where it will. Some people do this. It happened in Jerusalem. There were leaders there who capitulated and joined in the effort of Antiochus to impose his culture and rule on the city. They figured that the end was inevitable, and they simply got in step with the way things were going. This alternative is present in every age. It is present in ours. We can "drop out," believing that the current directions are inevitable and that the status quo is completely resistant to change. It's happening even now. A lot of people are saying, "What can I do? I am only a small ripple in an irresistible tide." The trouble with this alternative, however, is that, when you capitulate, when you throw in the towel, you become a part of the problem instead of a part of the answer.

We do need to remember that capitulation is not conducive to peaceful living. "Peace at any price" has never worked, whether we are thinking of nations or individuals. Shortly after World War II a man accused of collaborating with the Nazis excused himself by saying he was a soldier under orders. A few years later in an interview he admitted that he had not lived easily with his memories. "I now recognize," he said, "I must bear a part of the blame." That's where the person who capitulates always ends up. He can never say, "They did it." He must say, "We did it."

There is an old church in England which has on its wall the following inscription: "In the year 1653 when all things sacred throughout the nation were either demolished or profaned, Sir Robert Shirley founded this church. It is to his singular praise that he stood for the best of things in the worst of times."

It may well be that only those who approach life in a similar fashion ever find a true sense of inner well-being. There is considerable evidence that inner peace is born only in struggle. Every football coach is aware of this. A player sits on the bench, safe from all the knocks and bruises involved in the game. But the player is restless and keeps saying to himself, "If only the coach would let me on the field." Finally, the coach calls the player and gives him his instructions. The player's restlessness disappears. He is out there getting mauled and pushed around. But in the player's heart there is a tingle of excitement. Win, lose, or draw, he is at least in the battle. Peace in the struggle—can a football player find it any other way?

Not many people find exciting lives down the "drop-out" road. The reason has to do with the way we are made. When grave issues are at stake, neutrality brings little satisfaction. The people who live gloriously and meaningfully are those who have a cause, a purpose for living. There is some satisfaction in knowing that you have taken a side. The goal may take a long time to reach; but if it is right, no one need feel ashamed in working toward it.

The most important thought, however, in all of this is that even in this crowded world no life is unimportant. Every person can do something. That has always been true. When Antiochus sacked Jerusalem, there was one family who stood in defiance of his rule. In that family were seven brothers, and all of them were martyred. But the memory of those brothers remained. There came a day when the memory of those brothers rallied the city's inhabitants to action. The people stood again and reclaimed their city.

That kind of thing still happens. As a matter of fact, history is really the story of individuals. Look at any movement that has prevailed. Don't observe it at its crest when it has popular and widespread approval. Peel back the layers of history and search for its beginning. In almost every case there is an identical pattern. One person in a local situation decided to give himself to a cause with no strings attached. A few people gathered around that person, and the movement grew. In the beginning the effort was almost invisible. Often years passed before the transformation began to be evident. But in

68

the same way rivers start with brooks, great causes begin with what seem to be insignificant efforts. Movements start not with masses but with individuals.

A few years ago, three octogenarians were arrested as the leaders of a revolt in an old folks' home located in New England. The activist group seized the main parlor. Two officers suffered minor injuries during the disturbance: one was hit by a runaway wheelchair, and the other was jabbed with a knitting needle. The leader was an eighty-seven-year-old resident of the home who demanded that the old people be given a greater voice in running the home. "We've got a bunch of young whipper-snappers running things around here," he said, waving his cane. "We don't trust anyone under sixty-five." According to press reports, the old folks were heard.

Now, violence is seldom if ever the solution to any problem. It is true, however, that change can be effected by a handful of people, no matter what their ages, if they are actively committed. Two hundred years ago, fifty-five men penned a document that began with these words: "We hold that all men are created free and equal and endowed by their Creator with certain inalienable rights . . ." The document ended, "In defense of these truths, we pledge ourselves, our fortunes, and our sacred honor." Those fifty-five men and their cause prevailed, and the United States of America was born.

No one should count himself out or judge his life to be futile. We may not be able to do everything, but we can do something. It takes courage and a bit of thought. We may have to search a while before we find a place where our lives can count. But if we look long enough, have courage enough, and are willing to endure the struggle, even the least one of us can make a difference. People have been thinking that the world is going to hell for a long time. It hasn't. Someone always comes along to turn it back. You and I may be just the people the world is waiting for today.

A Sparrow on the
Housetop

LIVING WITH LONELINESS

A hundred years ago the most dangerous trail in
America ran through the wilderness from St. Jo-
seph, Missouri, to Sacramento, California. On April
3, 1860, eighty riders with two hundred horses attempted one of the most daring experiments of our
history. Across two thousand miles of treacherous
mountains, rivers and plains, the Pony Express set
out to link the eastern seaboard with the West
Coast. The Pony Express lasted only eighteen
months; it gave way to the transcontinental railroad.
Those twin ribbons of steel were soon followed by

the quivering wires of the telegraph and telephone. Still later came the airplane and the magic of radio and television.

It is fairly evident from these chapters in our social and technological development that people are driven by an inexplicable compulsion not to live alone. However, while we have conquered the geographical problem, we have not eliminated lonely hearts. One of our national religious leaders spoke recently on the problems afflicting contemporary man and woman. He said, "As I have traveled this country, I have discovered so many, many people who live in unbearable loneliness. This loneliness has its roots not in the isolation of space but in the alienation of people."

How accurate this observation is may be debatable. Most of us believe, however, that it is not totally wrong. When John Donne said, "No man is an island," he was not describing the way many of us feel. An ancient songwriter once declared, "I am as a sparrow alone on the housetop." Despite our crowded world, many people feel exactly that way.

This problem is particularly acute among older people whose families are scattered and whose circle of friends has been diminished by death. Their failing physical strength prohibits an active life style. The world goes by leaving them to spend countless hours alone. But older people are not the only folk who feel like deserted sparrows. Loneliness is at times the lot of everyone, young or old. The question is, "How do we cope with it?" To answer that question, we need to examine the anatomy of loneliness—the reasons we feel so lonely, and what we might do about them.

First, there is the loneliness of pain. There is an old folk song that has these lines:

> We must walk this lonesome valley,
> We have to walk it by ourselves,
> Oh nobody else can walk it for us,
> We have to walk it by ourselves.

These lines suggest that suffering can be a lonely experience. The proverb "Laugh and the world laughs with you, cry and you cry alone" is descriptive not only of the way it seems to be, but also of the way it really is. There is an inevitable loneliness attached to hurt, the sympathy of concerned friends notwithstanding. People who have been hospitalized understand this. The presence of friends and loved ones helps, but the night before major surgery and the days that follow it are lonely times. A sympathetic friend may assist in making such times easier, but no one—no matter how close—can suffer for us. Pain and the solitude that accompany it cannot be delegated.

This is true whether the suffering is imposed

upon us by careless and thoughtless living or by pain of unexplained origin. St. Paul was exactly right when he said, "Every man must bear his own burden." There is an old story told by Jesus about a boy who ran away from home. The wayward boy charted his own downfall. The solemn line in the story is this: "When he had wasted all, a mighty famine arose in the land; and no one gave unto him." The law of cause and effect works with relentless precision in our world. Sow a wrong seed, and you reap a wrong harvest. There is no escape from that.

Most of us can understand it when we get what we deserve. We may chaff under the load and complain about our lot, but at least we are not bewildered. There is, however, some pain and suffering imposed upon us that we do not merit. War, natural disasters, and the careless acts of others can make life tough and lonely. That kind of suffering we don't understand, and no one ever has. All we know is that such pain is real, and that it happens to people in spite of every effort to avoid it. When such hardship comes to us, it's difficult to bear. All of us walk this lonesome road once in a while.

While there is no way to avoid the loneliness of pain, it does need to be said that there is a way to endure it. In the scheme of creation, the Creator so arranged our world that no pain ever comes to us

74

without the strength to bear it. The interesting thing about this strength is that it comes to us only as we need it. Haven't you heard people say, "I didn't think I could make it, but I held on one day at a time and got through"? It helps a lot when you take hard days one at a time. People who come apart under pressure are those who try to handle everything at once. Suffering is best handled when you take it as it comes. If you start worrying about tomorrow or next week, you not only have to carry the load itself but also the worry and anxiety that come with it.

We need to remember, too, that every hardship can be made to serve a purpose. It's surprising how much easier a hard road becomes when you start asking, "How can I *use* this bad thing that has happened to me?" That kind of thinking takes your mind off yourself and gets to the creative use of hardship. The great people are not those who manage to escape pain and suffering but those who have found a way to use it constructively.

Second, there is the loneliness of failure. A children's television drama recently told about a child who one day brought home a report card with all A's. Her mother beamed with pride. The next day, however, the little girl discovered that the school's computer had made a mistake. She had received the wrong report card, and hers wasn't as good. That's a dreadful thing to happen to a child. What could she do? She remembered her mother's joy and pride when she saw the report card. How would her mother feel when she knew the truth?

Within that story is a reflection of an experience all of us have now and then. We often miss the goals we pursue. Every student is eventually confronted with a time when scores are less than expected. The young person senses keen disappointment when the peer group closes the circle and leaves him out. People in business know this feeling when the profit and loss statement comes out on the minus side. Failure is a devastating experience. It is also a lonely one.

We need to remember, however, that no one is prepared to live until he is prepared to fail. To miss the mark is the risk involved in any effort. Consequently, we need to prepare ourselves to face up to failure. This, of course, requires a philosophy, and such a philosophy may best be gleaned from a study of those who have experienced failure. Biographical research reveals clearly at least one thing: no failure need be fatal.

Mary Pickford once said that what we call failure is not "falling down," but "staying down." We may make mistakes, even serious mistakes, but there is always another chance. The biographies of the great people of the world suggest that conclusion to be valid. The people who "get it together" in life are not those who have escaped failure. Indeed, many of them know more about failure than they do about success. They have simply learned that every failure presents a new challenge and to start over is a new opportunity. A lot of the loneliness of failure could be dispelled if we would remember that no failure need be final.

Finally, there is the loneliness of principle. Mark Twain said that to be good is to be lonely. Of course, the great humorist's comment was made in jest. His gentle sarcasm, however, is not without truth. People who rise above the crowd, who hold to a principle of conscience, will be marked for solitude. This, too, is a fact of history. Those who stand for a cause must learn to stand alone. Remember Abraham Lincoln. His very name is synonymous with loneliness: the world remembers best his sitting in the White House brooding over the ruins of war. Churchill's finest portrait is the one that pictures him standing defiant and alone in his defense of freedom. The solitude of principle is always a possibility. The ground upon which a noble cause is defended is seldom held by a crowd.

Most older people expect to be lonely when they take a stand. Younger people, however, are often jolted by the reality of it. The great temptation is to back away, to fit the mold, to yield to the pressure.

It takes a sturdy heart to give one's allegiance to a principle. The reason is that those who do often stand alone.

There is no deliverance from this kind of loneliness. You either learn to live with the loneliness of principle or you go down. But there should be some strength for endurance in the awareness that there is something in the universe that is friendly to principle. Lincoln stated this thought in what is perhaps his best-known quotation: "I do the very best I know how—the very best I can—and I mean to keep on doing so to the end. If the end brings me out all right, what is said against me would make no difference. If the end brings me out wrong, ten angels swearing I was right would make no difference."

It is that kind of faith that makes the loneliness of principle bearable. The next time you feel like that lonely sparrow on the rooftop, remember Lincoln's words. There is something in this universe that finally sustains the right. If your cause is just, you may be lonesome, but the ground on which you stand will be firm.

Finding the Center

DEALING WITH INNER CONFLICT

M A N Y years ago, when Robert E. Lee was president of Washington and Lee University, a friend asked him which road to take to get to a certain Virginia town. Lee's reply must have been a commentary on the condition of the roads in his day. "It makes little difference," the general declared. "No matter which road you take, you will wish you had taken the other one."

Lee's comment on muddy, rough, and impossible roads may well have an expanded meaning. In recent years the word *frustration* has come into vogue in our language. The word does not describe a new human condition, but its widespread usage does suggest that this generation has had an overdose of the experience which the word implies. Derived from a Latin word meaning "in vain," frustration is that feeling we have when we strive to get somewhere only to find the path blocked at every turn. Most people are aware of this feeling in one form or another. For some, it is an intermittent experience; for others, it is a constant companion.

When you attempt to identify the causes of frustration, you discover there are many. Our business and professional problems often vex us, and in this uncertain world those problems will be perennial; we shall have to learn to live with them. There are also interpersonal frustrations involving family, friends, and acquaintances. These, too, are as inevitable as death and taxes. There are the pressures of time and calendar, the limitations of health and handicaps, and, to a greater or lesser degree, these afflict us all. But most often our frustrations are not external in origin. Many of them arise from within. While we may not be able to remove those frustrations imposed upon us from without, we can do something about those that arise from within. We are learning that, if we can handle those frustrations that are controllable, those we cannot control be-

80

come more bearable. Many techniques are being proposed to help in this direction. Sometimes, however, we overlook age-old ideas on the matter.

Much of our frustration, for instance, is the result of conflicting loyalties. There is a line in the Old Testament about some people who lived centuries ago. "In those days there was no king in Israel, but every man did that which was right in his own eyes." That sounds like utopia. Everyone goes his own way with no one to interfere or restrain him from his pursuits. But it didn't work well for that long-ago kingdom. Without leadership, the people floundered aimlessly. It was a time of great confusion. The trouble was that the people often had interests which were in conflict with one another.

What happens to people collectively also happens to individuals when they can't establish priorities. Charles Shedd tells a parable about a duck-hunter who hunted all day and bagged nothing despite the fact that ducks were everywhere. His companions, seeking to discover the cause of his problem, followed him to the blinds the next day. Their analysis of the difficulty was succinctly stated: "His trouble was that he was shooting ducks in general and not in particular." Life can be lived the same way. We can go off in all directions doing everything and seeking everything, but we seldom get anywhere.

It is this schizophrenic approach to life that does so many of us in. We try to accomplish goals and purposes that are incompatible. Examples of this can be seen everywhere. We want a reputation for honesty and integrity, and yet continue to deal off the bottom of the deck in our business ventures. We want to be loved and respected by other people, but by word and deed we repel them. We want homes that are havens of peace and serenity, and yet our behavior is a source of constant irritation and conflict. There is a time-honored proverb pointing toward a powerful truth: "Can two walk together except they agree?" Somewhere, sometime, you have to settle on a direction if you are going to handle frustration. It's a law of physics and a law of life. You can't travel in opposite directions at the same time.

Perhaps it is an awareness of this truth that leads us to a fixed and consistent conclusion: the quiet heart is the result of a "centered" life. The world will always remember a simple story told long ago by a great teacher. There was once a merchant who had diverse and varied investments. One day in his journeys, he found a "pearl of great price." So great was the beauty of the pearl that it became the focal point of the merchant's concern. He sold all that he had and bought the precious stone. Now the point of this story is not economic: it is not a suggestion that a businessman put all his eggs in one basket. The lesson here is that life must have a focal point.

George Fox, the great religious leader of another day, had a descriptive phrase. He often reminded his followers of the necessity of "centering down." By this he meant the coordinating of life under a single flag. Since our lives are immobilized when we attempt to go in two directions at the same time, it is essential that we choose a loyalty if progress is to be made. Fox's thought is valid when examined in the light of human experience.

It is a curious but simple fact of history that the people who have made the greatest impressions on history are not necessarily the people with the greatest talents. Many a highly-gifted person has gone to an unmarked grave with little to show for a lifetime spent on this planet. And people of lesser talents have changed the world. It requires a combination of ability and dedication to accomplish anything worthwhile. Often you hear someone say, "If only I had the time, I could achieve something." The fact is that we all have the same amount of time in each hour and day of our lives. The problem is one of selectivity. We have to make up our minds about our direction. People who change the world are those whose lives are dedicated to an all-consuming goal. They "shoot ducks in particular and not in general." Lincoln made up his mind about his direction and would not be sidetracked by peripheral matters. The same was true of Edison, Handel, Beethoven, and the rest. A dedicated and focused life is a powerful thing.

It is this "centering" of life that simplifies our existence. Singleness of purpose gives life a reference point against which to say "yes" or "no." We can't live a meaningful life joining every group and supporting every cause. The perennial "joiner" soon becomes disjointed in mind, spirit, and body. If we make up our mind about directions, center our lives on certain focal points, we are able to lead less distracted lives and are thus relieved of countless frustrations and anxieties.

The problem, of course, is one of choice. How do we choose a focal point? That question is not easily answered and there are many reasons. We are different individuals with different interests and talents. Also, all of us live in different circumstances. Some of us have greater opportunities thrust upon us by the accidents of birth and environment. When all of these factors are brought to bear on the decision about direction, we often feel bewildered and confused.

Young people in our day have a splendid and descriptive phrase. They talk about "getting it all together." What they are seeking is a way to focus their lives. This is their question: "When I consider who I am, what I have to work with, and where I am in life, how can I establish directions?" That question has no easy answer, and it would be wrong to suggest otherwise. But it is an important question. It may well be life's most crucial one. There should be at least one handle to help us find a solution.

Years ago a news reporter wrote a sentence in an editorial that a lot of people have since found helpful. "Every once in a while, everyone needs to stop and ask this question: 'If everything were taken from me that could be taken, what would I have left?' " That question moves to the heart of the matter. What comes first in our lives should be the last thing we are willing to surrender. Answer that question and a lot of things come into focus. It pits such things as health, family, friends, integrity, and character against other things such as popularity, fortune, and status. It puts the highest premium on timeless and proven values and quickly moves priorities into focus.

A lot of us spend our lives trying to satisfy hunger with food that doesn't last. We seek objectives which, when reached, seem empty and meaningless. Most of the time the futility of such pursuits would be evident if we would only ask, "Am I putting first in my life the things I would want to give up last?"

It's a good question to ask every day. When answered, a lot of anxieties and frustrations disappear. "Centering down" on direction makes life simpler; the bad roads get easier, and we don't have to live out our days wishing we had taken the other road.

When the Problem Is People

CONTENDING WITH PEOPLE

A professor in one of our great universities recently sent a questionnaire to the chief executives of some of America's largest corporations. The purpose of the questionnaire was to aid the school in planning its curriculum so that graduates might be able to cope with the practical problems of the work-a-day world. One of the questions asked those business leaders to identify the quality they believed contributed most to success. The responses were nearly unanimous: "W can teach almost any skill necessary for success in business provided the trainee has the ability to work effectively and efficiently with others."

The report from those businessmen is not surprising. The critical problem in most human endeavors is that of interpersonal relationships. So crucial is this matter that countless courses on the "people problem" are being offered in schools of management. Business, government agencies, schools, colleges, hospitals, etc., spend millions of dollars each year on public relations. How to oil troubled waters and facilitate harmony among people are of paramount concern in most organizations.

There is good reason for this concern. A lot of highly skilled and otherwise competent people find life extremely difficult for no other reason than their inability to get along with others. The problem is understandable. People are complex creations. We come in varying shapes and sizes and with all kinds of dispositions. We can be kind or cruel, proud or humble, friendly or distant, good or bad. At times we are pleasant and agreeable, while at other times we are impossibly irritating. It's a real problem for most of us—coping with other people. To suggest that solutions to this problem are easy would be dishonest. There are, however, a few principles that are basic. They are so incredibly simple that they are often overlooked.

We need to remember, for instance, that people

88

by nature are gregarious. When Daniel Defoe wrote his famous novel *Robinson Crusoe*, he referred to the unbearable loneliness that swept over the shipwrecked sailor when he finally realized he was on a deserted island. It took a while, of course, for this realization to come to Crusoe. His first days on the island were devoted to a desperate search for food and shelter. Once these necessities were provided, Crusoe began to feel a need to be with people.

Everything we know about mankind leads to the conclusion that people seek community. There is a story about creation in the Bible. The author of that story writes of the Creator saying, "It is not good for man to be alone." The significance of this observation has to do with the way we are made: loneliness is contrary to our nature. This fact is affirmed over and over in the great literature of the world. There are countless references to the brotherhood of man and the family of mankind. Indeed, one writer declares, "God has made of one blood all the nations of the earth." Even the casual reader understands the point of that sentence. By our inherent nature, we reach out for one another.

Now and then, to be sure, we discover someone who appears to be a "loner." But most psychologists believe that such people are not "loners" by choice. Indeed, the yearning for community may be even more acute for the "loner" than for other people.

Most people don't want to live alone. Solitary confinement is said to be the worst punishment we can inflict on anyone. The surest way to drive a person mad is to cut him off from all contact with other people. "It is not good for man to be alone."

Most of us who have "people problems" would do well to remember this. No matter how offensive others may be, at the heart of their nature is an instinctive desire to establish relationships with others. No one is farther from the truth than the person who says, "I don't care what other people think of me." We may say with some truthfulness, "I don't care what *some* people think," but we never mean *all* people. Few if any of us can endure the deserted island. We are driven by native impulse to reach out for others. It helps a great deal in getting along with others to realize that they, too, have the same desire.

We need to remember, too, that we tend to receive from others the treatment we direct toward them. That's really the point of the Golden Rule, is it not? "Do unto others as you would have them do unto you" is a time-honored maxim among us. Sometimes we mistakenly believe this instruction to be nothing more than idealism. In reality, however, it is more a statement about the way things are than the way they should be. Not only *should* we do unto others as we would have them do unto us, but others *will* do unto us as we do unto them.

Every physicist is aware of the law of cause and effect: for every action there is a predictable and dependable reaction. This law is always operative in creation. Seeds sown produce a like harvest. Every gardener works on that principle. Experience demonstrates that this principle also holds in other areas of life. Seeds produce their own kind. What we sow, we reap.

Someone has suggested that every person's world is a reflection of his own personality. That fact is readily discernable in human experience. Hate has a way of breeding hate, unhappiness breeds unhappiness, and a gloomy disposition tends to enlist that response from others. Seeds produce their own kind.

Anyone who studies "group process" is aware of this. Have you ever observed that in almost any gathering there are two kinds of people: enthusiasts and pessimists? Whoever gets the upper hand in such gatherings controls the atmosphere of the meeting. Discouraged people can destroy the spirit of an entire group, while the voices of optimism can change the mood in the opposite direction. There is a contagious quality of attitudes in interpersonal relationships. This contagion is operative in groups, and it works in one-on-one encounters. We usually get from others what we project toward them.

An awareness of this principle of cause and effect

should have direct bearing on our behavior toward others. So often we imagine ill-treatment from others to be a function of their personality disorders, and sometimes that's true. But more often than not the fault lies within us. It's a good rule to take an honest look at our own attitudes when we are having difficulty coping with others.

However, this question does arise: "How do we manage our attitudes?" There are many ways to face this problem, but essential to all of them is the development of understanding. There is a curious verse in an Old Testament book: "I sat where they sat and remained there astonished." Do you remember what was happening then? An ancient man was angry with his people because of their lack of courage and faith. One day this man decided to spend some time living where his people lived. When he identified with their circumstances and saw firsthand what they were undergoing, the man's attitudes changed. This usually happens when we "sit where they sit."

Many times our problem is an unhealthy obsession with self. We excuse our rudeness and irritability by saying, "I had a rough week," or "I've had so many things to contend with lately that I haven't been myself." We fail to remember that others can have rough times, too. Most of us would see a different world if we would give a bit of time and thought to understanding the circumstances of others.

There is an old parable about a father who became disturbed about the length of time his six-year-old son was taking to get home from school. The father decided he would make the trip and discover for himself how long it should take a small boy to cover the distance. The father settled on twenty minutes, but his son was still taking an hour. Finally, the father decided to make the trip *with* his son. After the trip, the man said, "The twenty minutes I thought reasonable was right, but I failed to consider such important things as a side trip to track down a trail of ants . . . or an educational stop to watch a man fix a flat . . . or the time it took to swing around a half-dozen telephone poles . . . or how much time it took for a boy just to get acquainted with two stray dogs and a brown cat. "In short," said the father, "I had forgotten what it's really like to be six years old."

There's a lesson in that story. What is it like to be another's age, to live where another lives, and to walk a while in another's shoes? We get wrapped up in our own world and fail to understand the world where others live. This lack of understanding breeds within us attitudes of contempt, envy, and irritation that are reflected toward others. These attitudes are then, by the law of cause and effect, reflected back toward us. A lot of us could live in a more pleasant world and find people more exciting if we could break this vicious circle. Cheerful, thoughtful, and understanding people seldom feel alienated from others. They usually feel at ease wherever they are and find a world of friends.

Riding the Top
MANAGING SUCCESS

ON November 22, 1963, John Fitzgerald Kennedy, president of the United States, was assassinated in Dallas, Texas. As the word of his death spread across the country, the whole nation went into mourning. Flags were flown at half-mast everywhere; radio and television stations cancelled their scheduled programs and replaced them with music interspersed with news related to the president's death. The following Sunday morning something interesting happened in our land. People attended their churches and synagogues in near record-breaking numbers. Indeed, some have said that more people attended worship services on that Sunday than on any comparable date in American history.

A few days following those tragic events in Dallas; an American theologian made an observation worth noting. "In troubled and uncertain times, most people are inclined to pray. The untimely and unexpected death of the president makes us acutely aware of our inability to manipulate the circumstances that control our destiny. Americans know how to handle success and prosperity but are completely bewildered by adversity."

Most counselors who listen to people for any length of time understand that theologian's point. The proverb "There are no atheists in foxholes" is usually true. In difficult times people are inclined to seek assistance. We look for help in places we never go when all is right in our little world.

It is not quite accurate, however, to suggest that Americans are well adjusted to success and prosperity. A prominent Southern psychologist speaking to his colleagues said recently, "Many of my patients are trying to cope with the problems of success. They are overcommitted, harassed by too many obligations, and feel guilty over the kinds of lives they believe they are forced to live. Many of them wonder if the compensations involved are worth the price they are paying." That's a generalization, of course, and generalizations are never completely true. There are, however, many people who fit the description suggested by that psychologist. It is not unusual to hear someone say of another, "He just couldn't stand prosperity." A lot of people do buckle under the pressures of success. That's always sad. Indeed, the most pathetic people anywhere are those who have everything to live *with* and nothing to live *for*.

We often imagine that the predicament of dealing with success is the result of the complexities of the modern world. We think that those who reach the top these days have to contend with a different set of problems than did their predecessors. That, of course, is not entirely true. Success has always been difficult to manage. Centuries ago there was a king whose life's story is one of rags to riches and back to rags again. As a young man this king had been a shepherd. A curious turn of events gave him a chance at the top. Brilliant and competent, he became the leader of his people. He led them to a place of prominence seldom equalled by any nation of the ancient world. But one day something went wrong with this young king. King Saul's life of prosperity ended in catastrophe, and he committed suicide. If you study the life of this king, you will discover an object lesson in how to handle success, because to do so, some things are absolutely essential.

First, the ability to handle success is dependent upon one's ability to identify valid and compatible objectives. In the early days of the automobile, it became apparent that laws were needed to control their movement. One of our state legislatures enacted the following statute: "When two automobiles arrive at an intersection, neither shall move until the other has departed the intersection." That law is said to be still on the books in that state, obviously unenforced. Enforcement is impossible. Actions inconsistent with each other result in paralyzing conflict. We never question that premise in the world of physics. Yet, in our lives, we often select contradictory goals.

This happened to that king back there. In the early years of his reign, he attempted to be a wise and benevolent ruler of his people. But as the years passed he became dazzled by the prospects of power, fame, and fortune. The conflict between these objectives is obvious, but Saul tried to hold to both. It is understandable that he finally came apart. You can't go down two roads at the same time. Saul forgot that, and his life ended in tragedy.

But even when you settle on an objective, it must be a proper one if success is to be meaningful. Studies have shown that in many instances the hard-driving, fast-running people do not know why they drive hard and run fast. In some cases the game is success for the sake of success. That never works, and the reason is that the top slot is an ever-moving target. As a result, these people never know when they have arrived. Remember that old description of the hungry tycoon: he only wants what's his and what lies next to it. People who haven't established objectives never know when they have enough. It wouldn't be so bad if such people found their dissatisfaction diminishing in proportion to the degree of success achieved. But more often than not the more they get, the more they want. Soon these people are overextended, and their lives become fragmented as they try to hold on to more than any one person can hold. The empires thus erected are built on sand, and they go down with a resounding crash. It's a time-proven axiom in history: power for the sake of power never lasts.

In one of the oldest books in the world, there is a striking sentence: "He that would be greatest among you, let him be the servant of all." That's not dreamy idealism but a hard and realistic description of the way it works. Fame and fortune are never valid goals in themselves. The great people who have ridden the top successfully are not those who sought "success," but who sought a great cause. Lincoln stands at the pinnacle of American history not because he sought success but because he championed a noble cause. That's the way it works.

Genuine success is achieving something lasting and useful. If fame and fortune come in that process, they are incidental to the central objective. Only those who accomplish worthy and important goals find fulfillment in their success.

Another aspect essential to achieving a satisfying success is remembering our dependence on those who helped make it possible. Our forefathers had a quaint but descriptive phrase: "A fellow can get above his raisin'." What they meant, of course, was that on the high tide of success it's easy to forget our indebtedness to those who helped us get there. King Saul did that. In earlier years he was humble, appreciative, and attentive to counsel. In later days he was proud, stubborn, and arrogant. His old friends were pushed aside, and their counsel ignored. Saul found himself lonely and filled with guilt. This often happens to people who forget where they came from. They lose their sense of inner peace, and in its place is guilt—guilt that comes from using other people as pawns.

It is said that Lefty Gomez, whose club held a World Series record of six wins and no losses, was once asked the secret of his success. He replied simply, "A fast outfield." Gomez only reported what has always been true. No one succeeds alone. The self-made person is a myth long since exploded by those who understand the interrelationship between people. To pass your benefactors in thoughtless in-gratitude not only builds resentment in interpersonal relationships, but is also destructive in achieving inner joy and satisfaction in success. The story is always the same. No one can wear the laurel leaves of victory in comfort unless he remembers to express his gratitude to those who have helped him along the way.

One final thought: success is always fleeting and relative. It's an axiom in sports that "Records are made to be broken." They always are. Old heroes give way to new ones. King Saul reached the top, but he couldn't hold it forever. He was replaced by a new king about whom even greater things were said. In the book that reports the achievement of these two kings, there is this somber sentence: "Saul slew his thousands, but David his tens of thousands." How time tarnishes success! Old idols fall and new ones take their place. Isaac Watts was painfully accurate when he wrote the following lines in "O God Our Help in Ages Past":

> Time like an ever-rolling stream
> Bears all its sons away;
> They fly forgotten, as a dream
> Dies at the opening day.

Success measured by external approval is too fleeting to be satisfying. A retired professional football player spoke to a father–son banquet in Asheville, North Carolina, a few years ago. Among other things, he said that twenty years before his name was in every newspaper in America, and he couldn't go anywhere without being recognized. "Now," he said, "no one knows my face, and few remember my name." Unusual? Not at all! Who were the news-makers of fifty years ago, or even of twenty years ago? Some of them we remember, but most of them we do not. The conclusion is obvious. Genuine success is not how the world feels about you, but how you feel about yourself. To believe in yourself, to know that you have done something to make the world a little better for someone else, is what warms your heart when you stand at the top and look back.

This is the way it adds up: success for the sake of success always leaves you feeling empty and guilty over the misuse of life. You soon discover that your exploits will be surpassed by those of another. The applause shifts, and another with more spectacular achievements comes along. When you ride to the top, you need to know that what you sought was worth what it cost to get there.

When You Lose a Loved One

COPING WITH DEATH

T H E R E was a man in Philadelphia a few years ago who received a unique award. The local morticians came together and gave Willie Hunter a certificate for attending some three thousand funerals. According to press reports, Hunter's hobby was attending the final rites of people throughout the area. For most folk such a hobby would be a depressing pastime. Funerals are not usually happy events. That's especially true if the service is for someone you know and love.

As a minister I am called upon to attend more

funerals than most people. I've never become accustomed to them. It isn't that I think of death as being at cross purposes with everything good and beautiful. Death is as much a part of the plan of life as is birth. My problem is that I dislike seeing people hurt. The loss of a loved one is a devastating experience, and there is no way around that.

There are many reasons death brings such a dreadful and troubled time. One of them is the sense of helplessness that comes when we face life alone. Many of us are terribly careless in our regard for loved ones. We do not prepare for our inevitable demise. We could do more to make the road easier for those who have to carry on when we are gone. A visit to an attorney, the arrangement of a will, and the honest sharing of our thoughts and interests with someone we trust could relieve a lot of unnecessary anxiety. We should never pass by these things lightly. Those who share the moments of grief with someone who has been left behind hear it over and over again: "I don't know what to do! We just never talked about these things."

There are, however, problems associated with death that lie beyond planning. No matter how careful we are in our planning, death is a time of sorrow and suffering for those who love the deceased. In such a time we look for strength and help. Friends are invaluable. The words "I care" never mean more than in time of death. Yet there are deeper needs that no human being can ever provide. To face the death of a loved one, more than any other experience, requires some inner convictions that are a source of strength. Here are three worthy considerations.

First, many people find consolation in the conviction that death does not have the finality we usually associate with it. Mark Twain once said that the only reason he wanted to go to heaven was because of the climate; most of his friends would be in the other place. The curious thing about Twain's observation is not its humor but the assumption that lies behind it. Unwittingly Twain was stating a belief that life has a dimension beyond this one world. Many people find such a faith illogical and unacceptable to an intelligent mind. They shouldn't. Hope of immortality is not just blind faith. The fact is, the more we probe and understand the scheme of creation, the more logical the hope of "more beyond" becomes. A full study of the arguments for immortality lies beyond the scope of this book, but two or three things can be mentioned.

C. S. Lewis, the famed British intellectual, presented an interesting argument on this very matter. He once stated that in the creative scheme a satisfaction is provided for every human hunger. If we long for food, there is such a thing as bread. If we are thirsty, there is water. If we have the capacity for love, there is such a thing as love. If, therefore, we have a desire for life that cannot be satisfied in the narrow limits of a single world, it is the only human hunger without possible satisfaction. "Is it logical," asked Lewis, "to imagine that the Creator would be so careful to provide for all of our other hungers and miss this one?" Dr. Lewis's argument bears some thought. The hope for life beyond is not illogical. Indeed, it may well be the most logical position.

We, of course, are accustomed to hearing the skeptics say that there is no scientific evidence of "more beyond." There may be a lot more than we imagine. Drs. Raymond Moody and Elizabeth Kubler-Ross have done some impressive studies with the dying that are not easily set aside. Even the scientific community is not quite willing to say absolutely that the grave ends it all.

Remember, too, that the belief in some form of immortality has been universally held by all civilizations from the dawn of history. Pascal, the French philosopher and thinker, once wrote this sentence: "God put the hope of immortality not in the human mind but in the heart." This was his way of saying that we instinctively believe in immortality. That belief is as old as the human race. We may talk ourselves out of that belief, but deep down inside the faith persists. John Greenleaf Whittier put it this way in "Snow Bound":

> Who hath not learned, in hours of faith,
> The truth to flesh and sense unknown,
> That Life is even lord of Death,
> And Love can never lose its own!

How did Whittier reach such a conclusion? He simply listened to the basic impulses of his inner spirit. If life is to make any sense, if there is meaning to struggle and effort, if Creation has any notion of justice, life cannot end in a graveyard. There must be "more beyond." Nothing in this universe disappears without a trace. Infinity is everywhere, and life is infinite. If you can believe that, then death loses some of its terror.

The second of our three aids to facing death is that many people find consolation in the belief that death is the doorway to life of wider dimensions. Wallace Hamilton uses a meaningful little parable about a bird locked in the prison of an eggshell. Its world is warm and secure. But one day the bird breaks forth from the shell. This process we call "hatching" or "birth." In a way, that moment of birth is a moment of death. The little bird dies in the world of the security and warmth of the eggshell, but it is born into a larger world of light, beauty, and adventure. Are not people similarly constantly dying and being born? The child leaves its mother's womb and is born to a larger world of childhood. After a while childhood gives way to the world of youth. Youth, then, gives way to adulthood. Every new world is a larger world. An old proverb states it well: "God never allows one thing to be taken from us without giving us the opportunity for something better."

Centuries ago a man had a message he wanted to give to the world. He had traveled most of the Roman Empire and planned to visit the rest. Indeed, in one of his journals, St. Paul wrote: "I must see Spain." Paul never got to Spain, but if he had, his name might have been lost from history. He became entangled in the wretched plan of Roman authorities to block him and his kind from speaking anywhere in the empire. He spent the remainder of his life in jail. In prison he could do nothing but write, and so he wrote. The world still reads his letters, and he has touched more millions through the written word than he could have by speaking. He lost one thing and gained something more. If this happens to us in life, why not in death? Could it be that while death thwarts us in the opportunities of this world, it may open for us greater opportunities in another?

Charles Allen has a lovely little analogy in his

book, *The Touch of the Master's Hand*. He pictures a college campus on the opening day of school. Parents drive up with their son or daughter. They help set up the dormitory room; they carry in the things necessary for college life. "But," said Dr. Allen, "if you watch closely, you will see a mama quickly wipe some tears when she thinks no one is looking." They are both pleased and sad. They are sad that one kind of relationship is gone forever, but they are pleased that their child has an opportunity for a larger life. "God never allows one thing to be taken from us without giving us the opportunity for something better." If that's true in the seen world, why isn't it true in the world of the unseen?

If we can believe that, then death takes on a different dimension. It doesn't relieve us of our loneliness. We do miss our loved ones, and that's the way it should be. It would be a lonesome world, indeed, if we were isolated from each other so that the loss of one would not be felt by the other. But it helps to know that, while we lose, our loved ones gain a life of wider dimensions.

Third and finally, there is consolation in the fact that with the passing of time, the hurt of death grows less and the lovely memories grow brighter. The human mind has its own built-in protective mechanisms. The mind is so made that it eventually comes to grips with sorrow and heals itself of almost unbearable grief.

Think for a moment. Did you ever observe how people look back on the past and reminisce about the "good old days"? Now, the good old days were not all that good. All of us know people who even think of the "Great Depression" as good old days. They forget about the hardships, the bread lines, the times they were hungry, and the long hours spent in trying to eke out a meager living. They remember the closeness of families and friends pressed together into deep ties by the nature of their suffering. "Those were the days," we hear these people say. What has happened? The mind has been at work romanticizing the past. It blots out the memory of bad things and highlights the good and the beautiful. It's a good thing memory works that way. If the mind held on to the bad and lost the good, we would destroy ourselves in despair and depression. We should not forget this when we are traveling through moments of great grief. Given time and a little help, the mind will adjust itself.

Counselors who work with grief-stricken people depend a great deal on this process. At the moment of death, grief can be almost unbearable. The world, bright with happy associations, suddenly becomes bleak and dark. With no beauty to be seen anywhere, people wonder if there will ever be sunny days again. But times deals with sadness and eventually places it in proper perspective. Grief diminishes and the hurt becomes bearable. After a while our souls are strengthened by the happy memories of the past. We discover a beautiful thing about life, which is that, though our loved ones are gone from us physically, they are still present with us.

Think about these things when "the bell tolls" for one you love. Death is not a cruel punishment imposed upon us by a cosmic prankster. Rather, it is an open highway to better things. Believe, too, that love does not lose its own, else the capacity to love is the most ludicrous joke ever imposed on humankind. And always remember that the night is inevitably followed by the morning. You may go through the darkness, but you will find the light again.

God Writes Straight
with Crooked Lines

SURVIVING MISFORTUNE

NEARLY four hundred years ago there was a king in England who wrote his name into the history of the world. It is possible that King James I of Great Britain will be remembered longer than any monarch ever to sit upon an English throne. In many ways, however, this king's whole life was marked with a pathetic record of greed, violence, and cruelty. Brutal in his suppression of opposition, it was this king who had Sir Walter Raleigh executed. James's last years were spent in morbid fear of death. He was so convinced that everyone was plotting against him that he was cheerful only when he was drunk. In the last years of his life, he seldom went to bed sober.

This king would probably have been forgotten as just another in Great Britain's long succession of monarchs. However, one day in 1604 he made a decision that would make him immortal. An Oxford scholar named John Reynolds suggested something to James I, and in an instant James passed a judgment that would result in the printing of the best-selling book of all time. Seven years later, in 1611, the book—which came to be known as the King James Version of the Bible—was published. More copies of this book have been printed than can be numbered, but the order to print it was given by the most unlikely person one could imagine. J. D. Douglas, a contemporary writer, commenting on this phenomenon, declared that the King James Version of the Bible is a striking reminder of a well-known proverb: "God has an astonishing capacity for writing straight with crooked lines."

Dr. Douglas's comment is not without truth. Often the greatest things in our world are brought about by the most unlikely people. No one can estimate the impact of the King James Bible. Translations of Judeo-Christian scriptures come and go, but the Bible of 1611 seems to hold its popularity and has for nearly four hundred years. The man responsible for it, however, can hardly be described as the one expected to do it. Indeed, it has been said that James I was the wisest fool in the history of Christendom. It is fair to say that God does have the "astonishing capacity to write straight with crooked lines."

There is in this proverb a lesson for life. All of us are the potential recipients of all kinds of misfortune. A poet once declared that not a day wears into evening but that some heart breaks. Anyone who travels a while on the highways of life will hit a streak of apparent bad luck. Most people are aware of this. Yet, when the bad luck comes, a lot of us are overwhelmed and hurt for a long, long time.

There is really no way to avoid such hurt. It is true, however, that remembering a few simple things can relieve at least a part of the pain and make the rest more bearable. Those things are implied in that old saying that God writes "straight with crooked lines." Consider two thoughts.

First, remember that everything that happens to us can be used for good. A few years back a lot of the "hit" tunes in our land were songs with deep spiritual overtones. One song that made the rounds of "pop" radio stations was entitled, "Why Me, Lord?" In the first few lines in that song the singer asks what he's done to deserve the kindness shown to him by Jesus. There is a picture in its words that describes most of us. Life is good to us not only because of our goodness and merit, but also in spite of our lack of it. God *is* able to write straight even with our crooked lines.

The truth is that often our blunders and mistakes can be useful and our troubles can become our blessings. Remember that well-known line from a wise man of the past: "My brethren, count it all joy when you fall into many temptations (trials), knowing this, that the trying of your faith worketh patience." This man is trying to tell us that our blessings often come disguised as troubles. History affirms that some of the world's most creative people have led the most tormented lives. Out of their suffering the texture of their contribution has been richly increased. Winston Churchill's graveled voice gave his words an even more powerful impact. Robert Louis Stevenson's sufferings made his writings immortal. Milton toiled through his blindness to immortal fame. Beethoven's deaf ears let him hear music the rest of us never hear. St. Paul, wrestling with his "thorn in the flesh," wrote letters that will be read as long as time endures.

God writes straight with our crooked lines. It helps to remember those words when we are struggling under some misfortune. In the hands of providence, our bad days become our good ones. The lovely designs of life are woven not only from the good threads but also from the dark and ugly ones. When we believe this, it's a lot easier to endure misfortune and calamity. God writes straight with crooked lines.

Of course, the question we raise is, "Can I really believe this?" Why not? Isn't the law of recovery written into nature? We view the violent spasms of earthquakes as tragic, and often they are. But it's a mistake to mark them off as all bad. Earthquakes and volcanic pressure build the mountains and form the streams that water the earth. Nature has a way of using bad things for good.

On the streets of a Southern city a while back, there was a mound of rubble. Someone had put it there and left it, dirty, ugly, and unsightly. But the moment the "litter bug" turned his back, nature went to work. A seed from a nearby plant blew into an empty can, a bit of soil formed from decomposed food, and the water from a spring shower began the gradual process of healing the ugly scar. A few weeks passed, and the scene was changed. Lovely honeysuckle had covered the trash and the fragrance of the vine's blossoms filled the street. That's the way nature works—turning scars into lovely things. And correcting bad things by using them for good. Of course, we can thwart the process, and by constant and unchecked carelessness make our planet uninhabitable. But scientists are continually amazed at how forgiving nature is. If given half a chance, it will grow a flower from a trash heap.

If such a tendency is believable in nature, why not in all of life? The same creative hand made it all. Surely it is reasonable to expect that, given a chance, this hand can make flowers bloom in life's bad places. It may take a bit of doing to find the flowers, but those who look for them say they are always there.

There is a second thought in that proverb, "God writes straight with crooked lines." Unlikely people can and do change the world for good. A part of what happens to us in bad times is that we lose faith in ourselves. We imagine that our misfortunes put us into places where we are useless, and that any worthwhile contribution is impossible. To believe this to be true is to forget the facts of history. No misfortune can totally eliminate our usefulness. Often it happens in spite of us.

There is a phenomenon of "serendipity" operative in our world. A lot of people looking for one thing find another, and many of us seeking to accomplish one thing achieve another. Was it not

Alexander Graham Bell who was looking for a way to aid the deaf and almost by chance invented the telephone?

It is said that one morning in 1888, Alfred Nobel, the inventor of dynamite, picked up a paper and read an account of his death. A journalist had made a mistake. Nobel's brother had died, and the reporter thought it to be the world-famed munitions manufacturer. Nobel read the story and saw himself as the world saw him—the "Dynamite King" who had made an immense fortune from explosives. He was identified as a merchant of death, and for that he would be remembered. Nobel decided to give his life a new direction, and he did it through the final disposition of his fortune. We remember him today not so much for his invention, but for the most valued prize given in his name—the Nobel Peace Prize.

It would be wrong to suggest that the invention of dynamite was a mistake. It has been used to enhance our lives with countless blessings even though at times it has brought us death and destruction. Nobel's story does suggest that splendid things come from unlikely places. It's the law of "serendipity" that keeps functioning in our world. God writes straight with crooked lines.

Most of us can look back on our lives and see places where the going was tough. We have been the recipients of calamity and misfortune. We may go down, but we should never let ourselves be counted out. There are still many opportunities to do something worthwhile if we but remember that God can write straight with crooked lines.

How to Know When
You've Done Your Best

FINDING INNER PEACE

N E A R the middle of the first century, an Alexandrian grain ship left the Island of Crete bound for the city of Rome. The voyage was long and dangerous. The sea was swept with violent storms. One morning, just at dawn, the ship ran aground on the beach of what is believed to have been the Isle of Malta. The 256 passengers aboard barely escaped with their lives.

Traveling on the vessel that morning was a prisoner, a Roman citizen, who had been arrested a few months before in a little Asian town and charged with civil treason. Had he been tried in local Asian courts, a prison sentence might have been imminent. But the prisoner was convinced of his innocence. Thus, before a verdict was reached, he asked that his case be moved to the highest tribunal in the ancient world; Roman law gave him the right to request this change of venue. And so he was on his way to Rome for the trial the morning the doomed ship ran aground.

The events that followed the shipwreck were interesting. The man who had boarded the ship as a prisoner was responsible for saving the passengers without the loss of a single life. Every traveler aboard that morning believed the man would be judged innocent before Caesar's court. They were wrong, however. The day the prisoner arrived in Rome, strange circumstances had the city in a turmoil. At first he was afforded a measure of freedom. Little by little, however, the web closed about him. We are not sure when or where, but there is considerable evidence that the man was executed without ever being brought to trial.

Sometime before his death, the prisoner wrote a letter to a friend. This letter has been preserved for us. There is in this letter the picture of a man who faced the end in perfect peace and tranquility. He knew he had made a mistake in appealing his case to Rome, but he wrote this: "I have fought a good fight; I have kept the faith; I have finished my course." St. Paul looked back at his life and was not ashamed. "I have," he said, "done my best."

Most of us wish for that confidence when we look at our lives. There are some timeless proverbs: "He always rests who has done his best," "Man's extremity is God's opportunity," and "God helps those who help themselves." The truths expressed in those proverbs seem right to us, but we are often haunted by a troublesome question: "How can we be sure we have done our best, that we have done all we can?" That ancient Roman prisoner felt he had done all he could and thus was at peace. We wonder how he achieved that assurance. That's a question worth considering. There are three steps involved in knowing when we have done our best.

Step one. We must recognize that our efforts are often limited by imperfect knowledge of circumstances. A well-known psychologist of another era once wrote, "The limits of human ability are unbounded. Most of us operate far below our potential. How can we ever know when we have done our best?" All of us sense the truth of that. Seldom do we use all that we have. Our brains function at only a fraction of their capability, and our physical capacities are far greater than we imagine. If, however, we expect to use our physical and mental facilities to their fullest, we will likely never know when we have done our best.

We fail to remember that the perfect utilization of our capabilities is dependent upon a perfect understanding of all circumstances. This would require infinite knowledge, and none of us possess that. We are, therefore, susceptible to mistakes. St. Paul made a blunder when he appealed his case to Rome. Had he stayed in Asia, he might have been freed by the lower court. Indeed, one of the judges in the local courts declared that he found no just cause for punishment. Paul must have realized that when he faced execution. "I have made a mistake in coming to Rome. But at the time the decision had to be made, it was made on the evidence at hand." That's the only way any decision can be made. You decide what you believe to be the facts and then act upon them. No one can do better than that.

Remember that old rhyme: "Of all sad words of tongue or pen, the saddest are these: 'It might have been.' " The picture here is of a person looking back at life and knowing that things could have been different. But do not most of us face that predicament? If we had full information on a circumstance as we made decisions, most of us could choose a better course. But life has a way of not revealing all the alternatives. We cannot know as much about the future as we know about the past. The best any of us can do is to survey the circumstances we see at the moment and then act as wisely as we can.

A few years ago a man burned to death in a hotel fire in Atlanta. Evidence suggested that upon leaving his room he was blinded by smoke. He made a guess on which way to turn and which hall to take. He guessed wrong and walked straight into the fire. Had he turned the other way, he might have escaped. The man, however, had no way of knowing this. He did the best he could based on the knowledge he had at the time. He had done his best.

All of us live under this dilemma. Many of our decisions must be made in a hurry, and many of them made by guess. We seldom know all the facts, but we have to decide. Whenever we take all that we know and act on that information in good faith, we have done our best.

Step two. It helps to know we have done our best if we ask no more of others than we ask of ourselves. Harry Emerson Fosdick used to say that whenever we face a dilemma about right and wrong, a good test to apply to the problem is that of sportsmanship. That is to say, would we be willing for others to play by the same rules we intend to use. That does help to put matters into focus, not only in ethical questions but also in other decisions. It's amazing the tranquility that comes to us when we know we have gone as far as we would ask others to go and given as much as we expect others to give.

A highly successful businessman, now retired, spoke recently to a group of young executives who were enrolled in a class on management skills. His wisdom was homespun but profound. "Young people," he said, "a manager always sets the pace for his organization. Employees seldom exhibit more dedication to their work than their leader does to his. Never ask anyone to do anything you wouldn't do, work harder than you work, or keep longer hours than you keep. Fail to keep these simple rules, and someone will soon be after your job." Now this observation is not completely true. Management requires more than dedication. Some skill at one's work is essential. But that retired businessman's thought is not without merit. People who have gone as far as they expect others to go seldom feel guilty about what they have done. It is true also that those who expect the most of themselves are likely to have the greatest sense of inner peace and security.

This was true of that prisoner who died in Rome on that long-ago day. It wasn't difficult for him to say, "I have done my best." Perhaps he had made mistakes and bad decisions, but at least he had gone as far as he would have expected anyone to go. Thus, he was at peace with himself. If we have given as much of ourselves as we would expect others to give, there is no reason to feel ashamed.

Step three. We have done our best when we have retained our self-respect. There is an old story about Senator John Tyler, who later became president of the United States. One day in the Senate, he had to decide on a crucial matter. His was the critical vote. The pressures upon him were tremendous, but they were contrary to his conscience. When his name was called, he voted his conscience. About that day someone wrote these splendid words: "Mr. Tyler slumped into his seat. There was silence in the great hall. Tyler then arose and walked out in the proud company of his own self-respect."

There is no greater possession than self-respect. To attain it, people have endured unbelievable suffering, even death. Empires have been yielded, positions of power have been relinquished, and fortunes have been given away by those who refused to surrender conscience. Three centuries ago an English cleric found himself in conflict with prevailing powers. One day, in defiance of what he believed to be a corrupt and degenerate system, he took a stand and was arrested for it. Placed in the Bedford jail for twelve long years, he supported his family by making shoelaces. In his spare time, he wrote books. On occasion he was offered clemency if he would yield his position and take a new oath of allegiance to the authorities. He consistently refused. We still remember his famous reply: "May moss grow beneath these eyebrows before I surrender my conscience." He didn't! The fact is that although he was finally released from jail, he died a pauper. He was probably at peace with few people except himself. The world has not forgotten that sturdy and intensely honest man. Two hundred years after his death, a statue was erected in Bedford, England, to honor his memory. One of his books has been translated into more languages than any other book except the Bible. It has been read in almost every part of this earth. John Bunyan's *The Pilgrim's Progress* is one of the most remarkable books ever written, and it was written by a man who was determined to remain at peace with himself at any price.

This isn't to suggest that fame always comes to those who hold to positions of conscience. The truth is that many an honest person lies in an unmarked grave. But that isn't really the point. As a minister I have shared the innermost thoughts of a lot of people. I have learned that the tranquil spirits belong to people who are not for sale. Many of them have paid a terrific price for their allegiance to conscience. But they are richer than a lot of people who handle fortunes and manage empires. They live in "the proud company of their own self-respect."

The world has come to appreciate the man who was executed that day in faraway Rome. He died branded as a criminal. We now know that the laws that condemned him were unjust. He knew it even then. But, in any event, he died at peace with himself, knowing he had done his best. He made his decisions on the best that he knew at the time. He never asked of anyone more than he asked of himself, and he held to his conscience when it would have been easier to go another way. Those who follow his example discover that his method works. They know they have done their best.

Dr. Fitzgerald is senior minister of the 3,700-member Centenary Methodist Church in Winston-Salem, North Carolina. He is the author of five other books: There's No Other Way, The Structures of Inner Peace, You Can Believe, Living Under Pressure, *and* How to Be a Successful Failure.